Just The Way It Was

Just The Way It Was

Tommy Dan Tims
Derrinageer, Ballinaglera
A true story of a traditional farm life in
County Leitrim, Ireland

A memoir by Thomas Gilrane

iUniverse, Inc.
New York Lincoln Shanghai

Just The Way It Was
Tommy Dan Tims Derrinageer, Ballinaglera
A true story of a traditional farm life in County Leitrim, Ireland

iUniverse books may be ordered through booksellers or by contacting:

iUniverse
2021 Pine Lake Road, Suite 100
Lincoln, NE 68512
www.iuniverse.com
1-800-Authors (1-800-288-4677)

Because of the dynamic nature of the Internet, any Web addresses or links contained in this book may have changed since publication and may no longer be valid.

The views expressed in this work are solely those of the author and do not necessarily reflect the views of the publisher, and the publisher hereby disclaims any responsibility for them.

Cover Design by Lorrie Dilts
Cover Photography by Patrick T. Gilrane
Editing by Wayne T. Dilts

ISBN: 978-0-595-44711-4 (pbk)
ISBN: 978-0-595-89032-3 (ebk)

Printed in the United States of America

This walk down memory lane is dedicated to my parents,
Thomas and Mary Ann.
Thomas was a gentle man who had a hard life and died before his time.
Mary Ann died the year I was born 1929.
It was my great loss for not knowing her.

Tattered & torn, this is the only known photo of my father.

Contents

Introduction

In 1947, an 18-year-old Tom Gilrane immigrated to the United States from the tiny "town land" of Derrinageer in Ballinaglera parish, County Leitrim, Ireland. As the youngest of three children and the second son, he grew up knowing that the small family farm would one day go to his older brother, Bernard. So when the opportunity came for Tom to emigrate to the US as a teenager, he left the only home he had ever known for what he hoped was a better life, as millions of other Irishmen had done before him.

He was, by any standards, successful. Tom went to work, served in the US Army, and earned his American citizenship. He got married shortly after getting honorably discharged from the service, and he and his wife Lorraine raised four children named Thomas Robert, Maryellen, Lorraine Theresa and Patrick Timothy, in New Jersey. Now retired, they have six grandchildren and no mortgage.

But his home parish in Ireland was never far from Tom's memory.

County Leitrim is in the north central portion of Ireland. Ballinaglera, the northernmost part of the county, is a triangular-shaped parish encompassing 23 square miles of hilly land and beautiful views. It is bordered on the west by Lough Allen, the first lake that the Shannon River flows through on its southern sojourn throughout most of Ireland, and on the north by the town of Dowra. There are 34 town lands in the parish, and seven families made up the "town land" of Derrinageer. None of those families could tell you when their ancestors built their 3-room stone cottages. Most of the farmlands had been handed down from generation to generation and, with very little record keeping outside of the church, the family histories are almost impossible to trace.

The days of Tom's youth were similar to those of other children growing up in rural Ireland in the 1930s, filled with farm chores both before and after school, regardless of the weather. And when some of the other families in the parish needed assistance, as they all did at one time or another, there was never a question of whether to help or not: they just did. It was a hard life, but not one of hardship. It was filled with work each day—sometimes backbreaking work for long hours—but it was work without complaint because it was a matter of providing for the family. It was a life without much money, but one where their needs were met, their family secure, and their friends were close by.

Tom had never known his mother. She died when he was just an infant. His father, brother, and sister—along with a grandmother for the first six years of his life—lived in the single floor, 3-room stone house with no electricity or running water. The central fireplace in the kitchen served as the sole source for cooking as well as heat. The 14-acre farm was just large enough to provide for the needs of the small family on a year-to-year basis, but was not big enough to be divided between the two brothers. Irish tradition dictated that the oldest son would inherit the family land, and Tom was the youngest. For the children, farm chores took precedence; school would last only through eighth grade; social interaction came through visits with neighbors—called "rambling"—or dances, sometimes held in someone else's house. And always with the knowledge that one day, Tom would have to leave. The big question for many years was where would he go?

When Tom finally got the opportunity to come to the US in 1947, he had no way of knowing at the time that he would never see his father or brother again, that it would be 25 years before he would ever return, and that his older unmarried sister would be the last member of this Gilrane family to live in the homestead that had been in the family longer than anyone could remember.

He has since returned to Ireland many times, bringing all four of his children back to the farm of his youth. The farmhouse he grew up in has fallen into ruins, and the land has been rented to other local farmers over the years who use the pastures for their cattle to graze.

Now in his 70s, Tom decided to document what life in Ireland was like growing up in the 1930s and 40s. With so little family history available about the generations that came before him, he was driven to record his youth in Ballinaglera as accurately as possible. This is his true account, written in his own words. In it he captures the stark necessities of farm life with a distinct Irish flair.

This is his story and it is, as he says, "just the way it was."

Wayne T. Dilts
July 2007

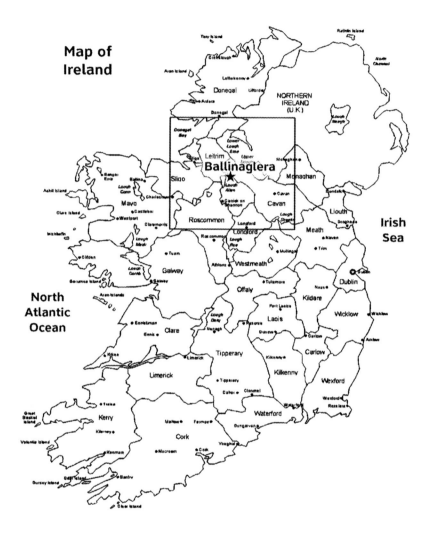

Map of
Ireland

NORTH
Atlantic
Ocean

Irish
Sea

Ballinaglera

1

Ballinaglera Parish 1929

§◊§

Family Names and Close Neighbors

If you never heard of a place called Derrinageer, you are not alone. A lot of people haven't, including many Irish. Derrinageer is a small "town land" located in the parish of Ballinaglera in County Leitrim, Ireland.

Ballinaglera is an Irish word meaning "Home of the Clergy." There are 34 town lands that make up the parish. While there are no actual towns located within Ballinaglera, the closest town is about a mile north of Derrinageer and is Dowra. Known as the first town along the Shannon River, Dowra is divided by the Shannon, which serves as the boundary line between County Cavan and County Leitrim. The largest part of Dowra is in Cavan on the northern side of the Shannon, and the smaller part is in Leitrim on the southern side. People there refer to Ballinaglera as a "village" but there are only a few businesses in Ballinaglera, and these are located near the church.

The two main business establishments are John Rynn's and Arthur Mulvey's. John and Arthur passed away years ago, but their families are still operating the businesses. Both places have the famous Irish pub and grocery store combination. These are the places to meet your neighbors for "grocery shopping" or having a pint.

I think the local people had a preference: some preferred Rynn's while others preferred Mulvey's. It was not often you would see a stranger in either place. Close to Mulvey's and the church was the Post Office. In my days there, Terry Cullen operated the post from his home. Terry passed away years ago but his family still operates the Post Office from the same house. There were a few more grocery stores in the parish but Rynn's, Mulvey's, the Post Office, and the church were considered the center of the parish and the places to be seen.

There are, or were, seven families that made up the "town land" of Derrinageer during my few short years there. Before my time there were many more.

Many families had the same last name, and to differentiate between them, the family was known by the first names of the last three generations to live in the homestead. We were known as the "Tommy Dan Tims": Tommy was my father, Dan was my grandfather, and Tim was my great-grandfather. Almost all families in this small "town land" were referred to in the same way with the first names of two or three generations.

In the "town land" of Derrinageer there were three families of Gilranes so using this way of identifying each made sense, especially when many of the sons and daughters had the same first names. The three Gilrane families in the "town land" were the 'Tommy Dan Tims", that's us. Our closest neighbor was Patrick and Linnen Gilrane, the "Patrick James Peter Terries" four generations of the men of that family who stayed in the old homestead. As far as we knew they weren't related to us. Patrick was the son of James and the only member of James and Mary's children to stay in the homestead.

They had many more children, and if for example his sister Mary stayed in the house and got married, she would still be known as "Mary James Peter Terry."

Another nearby family was Stephen and Ann Gilrane and they were known as "Stephen Tammy Tims," three generations of sons. My father always told me that we were related to Stephen but never told me how. I think the Tim mentioned in both families was the same man, but we have no records to prove it.

The next neighbor was Terry "Foggie" Gilrane. Terry was married to Kettie. I don't know what the word "Foggie" means. I think it is an Irish word. Terrie and Kettie had one son and his name was Tommy.

In most of the homes the eldest son stayed and married. The other children left, some to England or America, and some got married and raised families in neighboring town lands or other parts of Ireland. The father and mother would then stay on in the house with the married son or daughter.

Most of the houses were the three room thatched cottages like ours. This was not an ideal arrangement with the newlyweds and the parents in such a small place, and when babies came it became more difficult. This could be one of the reasons that most of the oldest sons who stayed in the homestead got married at an older age.

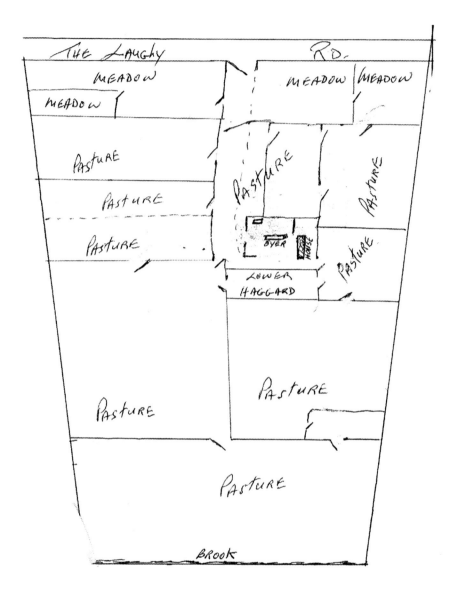

Hand drawing of the "Tommy Dan Tim's" farm
as it was used in the 1920s.
A farm is made up of fields that are referred to
by the functions they serve.

2

The Derrinageer Farm

~❦~

A Short History of the Farm and my Grandmother's Place of Birth

Our place in Derrinageer was not a large farm. It was less than 20 acres, sometimes referred to as a "three cow place" since that was about how many cattle the land could provide for. We always had two or three head of young cattle, and we always had a donkey, better known as an ass. We also had some chickens and at one time a few ducks. All the families had a number of chickens in them days. So when you were having a chicken dinner on Sunday, a trip to the hen house was as far as you had to go.

With the three cows there was always enough milk; most of the time there would be two cows to be milked at the same time. It was important to have milk all year, especially with children in the house. On those days when we had more milk than we needed, there were a couple of things we could do with what was left over. We could send the excess to the creamery in Dowra and sell it there, or it would be placed in large crocks inside the house where it would age. When the cream settled to the top, we would churn it to make butter.

The cream would be placed in a wooden churn. After it was churned for some time, butter formed on the top. The churn was then rocked from side to side—this caused the butter to stick together and float on top of the milk. It was easily removed with a strainer, salted, and placed in the butter dish. If the churn was more than half full you could get a few pound of butter each time. The milk that was left in the churn was called buttermilk and was also used to bake bread (called "fadge"), could be used as feed for the animals, and was very good to drink.

When one of the cows came in heat, we referred to in Derrinageer as "The cow's a bullin." You could hold off taking her to mate for a month or two. This way you could extend her milk productivity. Cows have a pregnancy that lasts as long as a human—nine months—and they stop giving milk a few months before they give birth.

When the cow was almost ready to have her calf, she would have been watched closely for a few days before. The old folks could tell almost to the day. We would check her before going to bed and if she was standing up and restless, that was a sure sign. As the night went on we would check more often, and when she became very restless we would stay with her. When she lay down, we knew the calf was coming.

When a calf is born it is normal for its two feet to come out first. We would sit down on a bed of hay behind her. Since the calf's two feet were very slippery, we would grab a handful of hay, put it around the feet, and start pulling. It took some time if this was the first calf the cow was having. After this first calf it went much faster.

Her best milk-producing time was right after the cow had a calf, and for a few months beyond, so the calf would be taken from her soon after birth. The cow could then be milked and the calf would be hand fed. As the calf got older, it was fed the buttermilk rather than the fresh milk.

Normally we would have three calves born each year, and they were usually kept for a year or two before being sold, giving the household additional money. With the size of this small farm, we were on a limited income. That was another very important reason for keeping chickens: they provided us with eggs. There was usually enough to supply us with what we needed in the house, and any left over were sold. If we had a surplus of eggs, say a few dozen a week, they were taken to the store and sold, and if we could send some milk to the creamery, even eight or ten gallons a week, this gave us extra money to pay for the groceries we might need.

The farm animals also provided us with the means to help our neighbors when needed. It was customary to help neighbors with a bottle of milk if they were short, and of course they would do the same for you.

Part of our land, usually two small fields, was planted with potatoes, cabbage, oats, turnips, and mangold, which is a vegetable much like the turnip. This gave us enough vegetables for the kitchen and some feed for the pig and the chickens.

A farm is made up of fields that are referred to by the functions they serve. The "pasture" is where the cattle feed or graze all year; the "meadows" are where the hay is grown and they are closed off to the cattle until after the hay is saved;

and the "fields" were where the crops are planted. Each field is fenced. In parts of Ireland, these fences were made of stone. In Derrinageer the fences are called "ditches" and are made of earth. Trees or shrubs are planted on top of these ditches so they become permanent. Alongside of the "ditch" is a "shough" (what the Americans call a ditch) for drainage. The field might have some depressions in them that would cause water run-off to go into the "shough" so there would be running water there. With the wet Irish climate there is always running water.

Now if your house is close to this running water, a well is dug to the depth of two to four feet and that is your household water supply. If there was a very dry spell and the well ran dry, they had to go to the nearest spring-fed brook or creek. At the bottom of our land there is a stream that is spring fed. It was a long walk back up the hill with two buckets of water, which is why we were grateful for the well we had.

Until long after I came to the Unites States, the town land of Derrinageer and all of Ballinaglera did not have running water piped in to the houses, which made bringing water into the house one of the daily chores. When some of these farmhouses were built hundreds of years ago, they were located near a stream or a spring well. Other homes, like ours, were built in the open fields.

Located close to each farmhouse were two buildings: the byre and the barn. The byre housed the cattle during the winter and the barn was used for storage year round. Today the farmers are building hay sheds with attached byres located some distance from the living quarters, but ours were built right next to the house. In the old, old days when all of the farmsteads were laid out, the byre was located close to the house. It was convenient for milking and foddering the cows in winter, and the old folks must have liked the smell of the cows.

The "haggard" was a small fenced-in field located close to the byre. When the hay was cut, it was brought in to the "haggard." Then the meadows are opened for a few months for the cattle to graze on the new growth, called "after grass."

At our little place we had two haggards, and we referred to them as the "upper" and "lower" haggards. They were both about the same distance from the house. The upper haggard, though, was closer to the byre and was better suited for foddering the cows in the winter. It was not well fenced and that was why we did not keep the haystack there. That was where we also stacked the turf and kept the chicken house. The lower haggard was where we kept the haystack and the oats. It had a good hedge of white thorn trees around it to keep the cattle out. It was also much larger than the upper haggard.

To make life more interesting in Derrinageer, and all of Ballinaglera when I was growing up, there was no electricity. What you never had you did not miss. Just think: no television, no radio, the only lights at night were the kerosene lamp, the turf fire, or the candle. If you had to go out to the byre to check on the cows, there was a kerosene lamp made especially for the outside. The outside lamp that we had was unique. I believe it came from the old horse-drawn carriages. It had a catch on the side that would hook onto the carriage and it had a round face on it that swung open when you had to light it, and there was a red reflector in the back. That lamp was one of the first things I looked for the first time I went back to the old place on my first trip home. I didn't find it. These lamps today are collector items. The newer lamps have a carrying handle and a round globe that makes a tight seal so the wind will not blow it out.

During the summer months, when the days were long, the men worked the fields till dark, so it was a short night before bedtime. However, the winter nights were long. It was during the winter months that the men went to neighbor's homes for a few hours at night after supper. This was called "rambling" and was much more fun than working. The main topics were the weather, crops, ghost stories, and the world problems, in that order. The women always stayed home and made the stir-about, another name for oatmeal or porridge.

Some of the older folks who smoked a pipe would share it when they were rambling. If someone came to our house and my father was smoking his pipe, he would take the pipe out of his mouth, wipe off the stem with his fingers and pass it over to the visiting neighbor. When the neighbor finished having a smoke on the pipe, he would wipe the stem off with his own fingers and pass the pipe back to my father. This was a common practice among the pipe smokers.

It wasn't done that way with cigarettes, though. Cigarette smokers might pass their pack around and let a friend have one of his cigarettes, but they did not smoke the same cigarette. I remember cigarettes being scarce during the War (World War II) and most cigarette smokers would pinch the light off when it was half-smoked.

Pipe tobacco came in solid bars, and John Rynn would cut it up into ounces. All pipe smokers carried a small pocketknife and they would cut just so much off their plug of tobacco, then scrape out their pipe and mix in the fresh tobacco, and then light it up again. It was a real project to watch.

These are the last pictures of the farmhouse still standing, where as many as 10 children were raised at one time.

3

Grandparents Daniel & Mary Gilrane

ഗ൫൪

The family of my paternal grandparents

My grandfather Daniel Gilrane married a girl from Glangevlin, County Cavan. Her name was Mary Fitzpatrick. They were known in Glangevlin as the "Cormick Tammies." She was a very kind and gentle woman.

The Fitzpatrick's home in Glangevlin was up near the mountain. The road to their house was not a good road. It was mostly covered with grass, what the Irish called a "boreen." From their home to the nearest store or church was a long walk.

The nearest town to Glangevlin was Dowra, which was over a one-hour walk. To find a girl this far from Ballinaglera wasn't easy. Grandpa Daniel must have had a matchmaker working for him.

This is how married life started for Daniel and Mary in their Derrinageer of the mid-1800s and their three-cow place.

Since I know my great grandfather's name was Tim (Timothy), why didn't I start this walk down memory lane with him? There's a very good reason, and it's sad. All I know about my great grandfather is his first name, Tim. I do not know his wife's (my great grandmother) name. I don't know her maiden name or how many children they had. The only one I know of is my grandfather, Daniel. Tim lived in the same house that the four generations of the "Tommy Dan Tims" that succeeded him did. This was the 1800s. In them days there were no pictures taken. The only place there might be a record is the Ballinaglera church, which was completed in 1842. There were no marriage license requirements or blood tests. So to get the information that went back this far is almost impossible.

I think the old house was built before his time, perhaps as far back as the 1700s.

Now to get back to Daniel and Mary, my grandfather and grandmother. Life could not have been easy. They raised 10 children in this small house. They had three boys, and their names were Patrick, Timothy, and Thomas. Patrick was their oldest child. The seven girls' names were Annie, Catherine, Ann, Mary, Alice, Mary Edwin, and Teresa Agnes. These were the 10 living children of Daniel and Mary Gilrane. Teresa Agnes told me that they lost four children, which would have made it 14 children. This was before prenatal care, before running water, before electricity. A neighbor helped with the childbirth. She was called a midwife. She had no training in this field; her only training was life experience.

The old Irish tradition was that the farm was handed down from one generation to the next. Take our place and family for example. My father had 14 in his family. With a large family like this the oldest son has to get a job when he gets out of school. The first few years are usually spent helping other farmers for a few shillings a day, and if they don't pay you, at least you get fed.

Seventeen or eighteen years old was the age when the oldest boys left home for the States or England. Now if there was a small family with only two or three children, chances were that they would remain home. There was always some work on your farm or helping neighbors. The same situation existed for the girls. If there were two or three girls in the family, some of them would leave. If there were relatives in the States, those relatives would help them get there. Some of the girls stayed home in Ireland and got married. With the very large family of my grandparents, Daniel and Mary, when the children became old enough to work, there was no choice: they had to leave.

The Irish custom was that the oldest son stays home and gets the old place. My father was not the oldest but with such a large family, this was not possible. My uncle Patrick was the oldest son and he went to live in England. There was another brother, Tim, and he came to live in the States. Ann, one of the sisters, married Myles McNiff of Upper Annagh, and she became Jim McPadden's grandmother. All of my father's other sisters came to live in the States. So the only one left in the place was my father, Thomas.

So when I left, my brother Bernard and sister Teresa were left to live in the place with my father. After some time, Teresa went to England. This did not work out for Teresa, however, and she returned to the farm. If Bernard had lived, he would have eventually married. It was never an easy life on such a small farm, yet four generations (that we know of) made it work. Where would I be today if I was the one to stay? There is no answer.

So the Irish tradition of the oldest son staying home and getting the place for his own sometimes just didn't work out.

Patrick was the oldest and by Irish custom, the oldest son stays in the place when he gets married. In Patrick's case, this would have been impossible with nine living brothers and sisters still in the house. Patrick left home as a very young man and went to England. From there he came to the United States and, as far as I know, Patrick never returned to Derrinageer. Patrick got married in the States to a woman named Dolly. They had two sons, Harry and James, as well as daughters, but I don't know how many or what their names were. Harry and James married and had families of their own. Over the years we have lost all contact with them.

Daniel and Mary's second son was Tim. He came to the United States and lived in the same rooming house in Brooklyn, New York most of his life. He became very close to a lovely family that owned the house, and they treated him as part of their family. Tim never married. I met him only a few times. I went with my Aunt Teresa Agnes to Tim's funeral in the early 1950s. Sad to say that's all I remember about my Uncle Tim.

Six of Daniel and Mary's daughters came to the States, and three of them went into the convent. They were Sister Alice, Sister Mary Edwin, and Sister Teresa Agnes. Sister Alice died in 1918 and was buried in Indiana. I don't know what order she was in. Sister Mary Edwin was with the Sisters of Charity and was a schoolteacher. She died in Saint Raphael's Hospital in Connecticut in 1954 and is buried in the College of Saint Elizabeth cemetery in Convent Station, New Jersey.

Sister Teresa Agnes was over 80 years old when she stopped teaching and retired to The Villa at Convent Station, New Jersey. She was 102 years old when she passed away in 1987, and is also buried at Convent Station, in the College of Saint Elizabeth cemetery.

Catherine lived in Jersey City, New Jersey. She married Lester Champlion and they had one son. His name was Lester. Catherine passed away some years before her husband Lester. They are both buried in Holy Name Cemetery in North Arlington, New Jersey. Their son Lester married a girl from Jersey City whose maiden name was Noonan. They were married in Saint Aloysius Church in Jersey City and moved to Smithtown, Long Island. After that we lost contact. They had a large family but I don't know any of them.

Aunt Mary married a man named Tom Dolan and they had two children, Gene and Margaret. I was told that at one time Tom and Mary owned and operated a candy store in Bayonne, New Jersey. Mary and Tom lived in Jackson

Heights in a lovely apartment. Tom was the first to die. Mary passed away some years later. Their daughter Margaret married Jack Littleton who was a ferryboat captain on the Hudson River from Staten Island to Manhattan. They had no children and are both retired now living in Amityville, Long Island. Gene married a girl named Merriam ("Mim"). They had two boys and three girls. One son was a police officer in New York City and the other was a teacher. They are both married and have families. I have not seen them in years. I am not sure if the girls are married. We exchange Christmas cards with Mim and Gene. They live in Little Neck, Long Island.

Aunt Annie married a man by the name of Cassidy, and they had no children. Annie worked as a dietitian for a hospital and lived in Jersey City for many years. Her husband died before I came to the States in 1947. After Annie retired, she moved to Hialeah, Florida. She passed away in 1956 or 1957 and is buried in Hialeah. Annie left us some Roger Brothers silverware, not a full set, and $500.00.

After I came to this country, Aunt Annie took me to Boston to see an old man by the name of Patrick Skinner. She told me we were related to Patrick but I don't remember how. I do remember he gave me $20.00. That was the only time I met him.

When I was very young, before school age, Annie and the two nuns (Teresa Agnes and Mary Edwin) were home in Derrinageer for a visit. Annie had a small red cosmetic case with a zipper that went all around. In it was bottles of nail polish. Well, one of us (probably me) got the case open and some of the nail polish got spilled. She was not happy. The things we remember.

Of the 10 children of Daniel and Mary, two remained in Ballinaglera: Aunt Ann and my father, Thomas.

Aunt Ann married Myles McNiff of Upper Annagh, another town land in Ballinaglera, bigger than Derrinageer. They had a small place like ours, probably a two or three cow place with the three-room thatched cottage. The Upper Annagh Road went through their land. As you came from Dowra, their meadows were on the left. The house was one field off the road and the pastureland went all the way back to the River Shannon.

Myles was a lot older than Ann. I remember Myles sitting by the turf fire smoking his pipe. I never saw him out working the fields. I was very young when Myles died, and I don't know what year it was. Two sisters of Myles lived across the Shannon River in New Bridge. When they got old and could not care for themselves, they moved in with Ann and turned over the farm that they had in

New Bridge to her. Ann is buried in Fahy graveyard on the shores of Lough Allen.

Myles and Ann had two children, Tommy and Mary Ann. Tommy was the oldest. He liked to smoke the pipe and have a pint of stout I remember they had an old donkey, and when he got tired he would lay down on the road. Tommy had a bell that he carried. He would ring that bell trying to get him back up. Tommy came up to the mountain with us one spring and cut turf. From Upper Annagh to the top of the mountain was a two-hour walk. To bring the turf home was a big job with a few donkeys. In the early 1940s, Tommy got sick and died. I don't know what was wrong. I think the doctor came to see him. The closest doctor would have been in Drumshambo, that's about 20 miles away.

Mary Ann married the next-door neighbor James McPadden. When they got married, it also joined the two farms together making it one big farm. They had two boys, Jim and Frankie.

In memory of Councillor Jim McPadden whose untimely death on March 12 2004 is deeply regretted. Jim served the local community with tireless dedication.

Mary Ann, in not too many years, had five funerals from her home. Her father Myles, her mother Ann, her brother Tommy, and her two aunts. That's not easy to take for a young woman. Mary Ann's son Jim built a new home where the old one was and a small warehouse close by. Jim married a girl named Carmela and they had two boys. They lived most of the time in the town of Sligo. Jim died in 2004. A monument was erected to him in Dowra. Carmela is a nurse and works in a hospital in Sligo. Frankie is not married. He lives at home and works the farm.

Of the 10 children of Daniel and Mary, the one who stayed in the homestead was my father Thomas. I don't know if he was the youngest, or where he fit in among the ten children, but he was the youngest son. My father married a girl from Glangevlin. Her name was Mary Ann Rountree. There must have been something special about the girls from Glangevlin. My grandfather Daniel and my father Thomas went there to find brides.

Daniel was not old when he died in 1916. My grandmother lived 20 years after him, but I don't know how old she was at the time of her death.

Bernard

Bridget Theresa

Thomas

The last generation of children
to be raised at the "Tommy Dan Tims"

4

The farm life—1930s

❀

My Father and Mother
Thomas and Mary Ann on the Farm

Thomas and Mary Ann had three children. Their firstborns were twins, my brother and sister Bernard and Teresa, on February 2, 1926. The little thatched three-room cottage was getting crowded again. My grandmother Mary was still living there and was, I am sure, a big help with the twins. After raising 10 children of her own, there wasn't much she didn't know about raising little ones. Even though she was old, she could watch us children and do the cooking.

Bernard and Teresa were almost three years old when I was born on January 28, 1929. (In later years, I was always told that I had been born on the same day as Bernie and Teresa. It wasn't so that we only had to celebrate one birthday. Birthdays were not celebrated in Ireland, at least not in my time or in my house.) Later that year my mother, Mary Ann, got sick. She was taken to the hospital and was not allowed to see Bernard, Teresa, or myself. I was told years later that she had tuberculosis. She passed away in 1929 before I was a year old. As I mentioned before, there were no pictures taken at weddings or christenings, so I don't know what my mother looked like. Now life became a lot harder for my father with twin three-years-olds and a baby one year old. It was great for him to have my grandmother there to help.

I do remember my grandmother. She wore a strange little bonnet to church every Sunday with two straps that tied under her chin. She used to clean and brush that bonnet every week. When she said her prayers at night, she always finished by saying, "And for poor Alice that died in the convent." She also said a prayer that she would die during the day. That prayer was answered when she passed away in the afternoon in 1936, 20 years after her husband Daniel.

19

It must be very hard for any man when he loses his wife. With three small children it is much more difficult. Now we must remember where we are. It's Derrinageer in the 1930s on a small farm. Three young children can be very demanding, and take a lot of your time, but they become even more demanding when added to the responsibilities of tending to three cows, with some young cattle, an old donkey, and some chickens.

The routine of the day started early in the morning with everyone expecting breakfast. The first thing was to start the turf fire. It often took a while for the turf to light and then get hot enough to cook on. Then, if we did not have water in the house, a trip to the well was next. The kettle was filled and put on the fire and while the kettle was boiling, we had to make a trip out to the byre to fodder the cattle. During the summer the cows didn't need to be foddered because they were out in the pasture day and night with enough grass for them to eat.

The cows were usually milked before breakfast. Now to milk the cows when they were in the fields, we would take the pail and the small milking stool. When we found the cow to be milked, the small three-legged stool was placed at her right side. We sat down and started milking. The cow would just stand there. She would also stop grazing till we were finished. The only thing we had to watch was her tail. All cattle usually travel with their own army of flies and when the cow uses her tail as a fly swatter, we could get hit in the face.

When we finished milking the first cow, she would walk away and start grazing. The other cows would be close by because they usually stayed in a group. Sometimes when the cows were giving a lot of milk, one pail wouldn't be enough. If we were to fill the pail to the top, it wasn't easy to carry back without some milk spilling. During the milking, sometimes the cat would join us, especially if we were milking in the byre. By turning the cow's teat sideways we could hit the cat with a stream of milk right in the face. That old cat would stand there licking his face as fast as he could.

On the way back to the house with the pails of milk, we would check the smoke coming from the chimney. If there was a lot of smoke it meant that the fire was not well lit yet. If there was just a trickle of smoke, the fire would be blazing and the kettle would be near boiling.

Checking the chimneys of our neighbors was another way to tell if it was early or getting late to leave for school. A look at the chimneys at Stephen Tammy's, Patrick James Peter's, Tom Trush's, or Peter Cremer's was a good indicator of the time. Lots of smoke meant they were just getting up and starting the fire, so it was too early to leave for school. Very little smoke meant the fire was blazing, that they had been up for a while, and it was getting late. For a few months in the summer when school was out, time wasn't important.

The angelus bell rang three times a day: at 9 a.m., noon, and 6 p.m. The bell was rung by Myles "Lacky" Loughlin. There is a long rope coming down on the left side of the door entrance. Whatever our work was, at the ringing of the bell, we would stop and say the angelus. However, if I were milking the cow, I would finish milking, and then say the angelus. If we heard the 9 a.m. bell on a school day, we knew we better hurry.

Back in the house after foddering and milking the cows, we had our breakfast, which was oatmeal most of the time. Sometimes we just had tea with bread and butter. After breakfast, the chickens were let out of their coop and fed. Their morning feed might be mashed potatoes with some corn meal mixed in. The corn meal was called "Indian buck." It was good for the chickens, and we could also make porridge from it. The pig was fed twice a day and got much the same food as the chickens. If we had young calves, they were waiting to see us. If they were very young, they got fresh milk. If they were a few months old, they would get skim milk or butter milk.

If there were a few people helping out, the morning work got finished pretty fast, but when we were all young children, my father had to do it all, especially the outside work.

Lunch was never a big meal: simply bread and butter with a cup of tea was the usual. Dinner was the big meal of the day, and we always had potatoes. A big pot of potatoes would be boiled and what wasn't eaten would be fed to the chickens and the pig. With the potatoes would be cabbage and bacon. Sometimes on Sunday as the chicks were getting older we would have a young rooster for dinner. There was only one rooster needed to be with the hens, so any young roosters that were hatched would be a Sunday's dinner when they got a little older.

The pot that we boiled the potatoes in was big and round with three legs. It would have taken 25 pounds to fill it. It was made of cast iron and when the water was added to the potatoes it was very heavy. This big pot had two ears on the side, where the pot hooks fit into. It had a heavy cast iron lid.

The crook was an iron fixture that hung over the fire that we would hang either the pot, the oven, or the pan on, depending on what we were cooking. The crook could be raised or lowered to control the cooking temperature.

The oven we had was also made of cast iron and was used a lot in the kitchen. When we think of an oven today, we think of it as a part of the kitchen stove with controls to regulate the temperature. The oven we had was not part of a stove but was a kitchen utensil about 18 inches around and did not have the belly in the center like the pot. The oven was six to eight inches deep, had the same three legs as the pot, as well as the two ears or hooks on the sides to hang it on the crook over the fire. Our oven was used for baking bread, making the porridge, boiling the chicken, and cooking most meats. The oven had a cast iron lid (heavy) that made a tight cover on the top.

When baking a loaf of bread, the turf fire would have to be glowing bright. The dough was placed in the oven with the lid on. It was then hung over the fire and hot coals from the fire were placed on the lid. The frying pan was also of cast iron and was sometimes used to make bread. The bread on the pan was cooked on one side for a while and then it would be turned over to brown on the other. It would not end up to be as thick as the bread baked in the oven, but this bread was very tasty, especially when we got to eat it hot with butter and a mug of buttermilk.

The pot, the oven, and the pan each had hooks on the side for hanging them over the fire. These hooks were called the "pot hooks" that fit into all three of these utensils. So if we were boiling potatoes in the pot, baking bread in the oven, or frying bacon on the pan, we had to use the "pot hooks" to hang them on the crook over the fire. Only one of these utensils could be hung on the crook at a time. The kettle was also cast iron and heavy.

There was a stone retainer on each side of the fire that was called the "hob" and it kept the fire contained to the grate area. We could place a kettle on this hob to keep the water warm. If we were out working the fields, and came in wet and cold, we could also warm our feet on the hob.

While we are still talking about the kitchen, I must mention the bucket, the can, and the ponger. The old bucket was used for many things like feeding the pig or the chickens. It was also used to feed the calves that were still on milk. In the summer when the weather was hot and dry, if the water in the well was low and the cattle didn't have enough to drink, we would go to the stream that was spring fed at the bottom meadow by Stephen Tommy Tim's land and bring buckets of water to the cattle. This did not happen often as most summers were not that dry. As you can see, the bucket was important.

We did not have a problem without electricity as we never had a big supply of food on hand at any one time. The cows were milked every day and all of the milk was used in one way or another. If we were putting milk away to be churned for butter, it was kept in a big crock for several days until it became thick and the cream rose to the top. If we were sending extra milk to the creamery, it had to be kept cool. There was a spot in the shough that was shaded from the sun and where the water ran all the time. The milk can that went to the creamery held about ten gallons and was placed in the running water. The extra milk was added to this can until the day that Pat McTiernan was going to the creamery. On that day we would haul the can up to the side of the Loughy Road for Pat to pick up.

The potatoes, cabbage, and turnips did not need refrigeration. We had two closets in the kitchen, and each one was called a "press." The press next to the dresser was where we kept the butter, eggs, and bread. We did not have any left-over meat that I can remember. Most of it was eaten when we had it for dinner. The food kept well because it was never as hot as it is here.

The potatoes were left in the field where we had dug them up. If they had been grown in a field that was far from the house we would bring them to one of the haggards or another spot closer to the house where they would have to be covered with rushes and six inches of dirt on top to keep them from freezing in the winter. We brought them in as we needed them, usually enough for a few days at a time.

In the spring when the weather got warm, one of the things I always looked forward to was taking off my shoes and going barefoot. Well, when you spent the day barefoot in the pasture, your feet would get pretty black with dirt. When it was time for bed, one of the requirements was that the feet get washed. You guessed it: out came the old bucket with some hot water.

The can, on the other hand, got more respect. It was used to milk the cows and could hold about two gallons. The bucket was made of galvanized metal and the can was made of tin. So the can was not as strongly constructed and could not be used for the same chores as the bucket.

The ponger was made of tin and was the size of a large mug with a handle on the side.

During this time, the 1930s, we had people that traveled around the area. They were called the "tinkers" and they had no real home. They lived on the roadside in horse-drawn caravans. The men were good tinsmiths and made the cans and the pongers. The women went from house to house asking for hand-outs.

The kitchens of these days also had a dresser and cabinets. The cabinets were called "a press" and were used for food storage. Today they also have what is called a "hot press" which is also a cabinet but it has some type of heat in it and can be used for drying clothes. The dresser was used for displaying or storing the dishes. It had three or more open shelves. On the bottom half were two drawers and below that there were two cabinets. The dresser and the press were a part of most kitchens. Our kitchen table was the type that folded up against the wall when not in use.

During the winter months the cows were kept in the byre at night. They were tied in place with a rope around the neck. The end of the rope had a ring on it that rode up and down on a stake as the cow moved. In the morning, they were foddered and milked. Then after breakfast, they could be let out to graze. In the late afternoon they would come back by themselves and when the byre door was open, they would walk to their own place and stand there. After supper they were milked and foddered for the night.

Most winters we had a few young cattle, two and three year olds that stayed out all the time. They were fed hay (foddered) morning and night. The old ass (donkey) was usually out all winter and he had to get some hay.

It was not an easy life, even when both parents were alive. It was harder for my father because he had to take care of the cattle, milk the cows, and feed the chickens and pig by himself, along with the cooking and cleaning and the wash. Today in Ireland all of the cooking is done with Propane gas but in those days it was only with the turf or a wood fire in the grate.

Fahy Graveyard
overlooking Lough Allen

In
Loving Memory of
DANIEL GILRANE DIED 1916.
MARY GILRANE DIED 1936.
MARY ANN GILRANE DIED 1929.
THOMAS GILRANE DIED 1949.
BERNARD GILRANE DIED 1967.

R.I.P.

The Family Stone

St, Hugh's Church in Ballinaglera

5

Fahy Graveyard

❧❦❧

Inch Island, Lough Allen, and St. Hugh's Church

The graveyard we use is by Lough Allen and is known as Fahy. The oldest grave-stone reads "Pray for the soul of Nancy Karr who departed this life April 5, 1796, aged 37 years." Fahy graveyard was founded in 1735 when burials were stopped on Inch Island, which is in the middle of Lough Allen. Before Fahy was started, the deceased were taken out to Inch Island to be buried. I sometimes refer to Inch Island as Patsie's Island because the name of the man who owned it in my time was Patsie Foley.

Fahy graveyard is about one acre but over the years a lot of people have been buried there. The Gilrane families have four graves that were assigned or given to the family name, and the four families that are buried in these separate graves are the Tommy Dan Tims (our family), the Patrick James Peter Terries (Patrick and Linnen's family), the Stephen Tammy Tims (Stephen and Ann's family), and the Tommy Terries (Tommy and Bridget). Counting just husbands and wives and going back three and four generations, that comes to 27 people that are buried in these four graves.

In the old days, most families did not get markers or head stones for their graves because of the cost. Unlike the graves in the United States, there is no cement vault that the casket is placed in and because of this the coffin, which is made out of wood, only lasts a few years.

There is also a graveyard by the church that goes all around it. There are a lot of people buried there that do not have grave markers and for the same reason, people did not have a lot of money in them days.

Inch Island is about eight acres with trees growing all around on the lake side. The island is about a mile out on our side of the lake. Some years ago the level of the water in the lake went down considerably, and at one section of the island there was a sand bar and it was possible to walk to the island after crossing the fields at the end of Lower Annagh Road. The only way to get to the island now is by boat, as the water level in the lake is much higher.

The ruins of an old church still remain in the center of the island. For many years, this was the parish burial grounds. The deceased were taken to the island by boat, and if the lake was too rough in windy weather, the family had to wait.... sometimes for days. There are no headstones or grave markers on the island and to my knowledge there is no record as to how many people are buried there.

My wife and I made a trip to the island when the lake was low. It was a long walk through the fields to the sand bar that led to the island. In the ruins of the old church, in crevices in the walls, were human skulls. Archaeologists have explored the island but I do not know what their findings were.

I went fishing one day when I was a boy where the Shannon River feeds into Lough Allen. It was always a good spot to catch a few fish. Could be they liked the water from the mountain coming into the lake. I had an old homemade rod made out of two long sticks. The strongest stick you held on to. The other piece was not as thick and had a little snap to it for casting. Both pieces overlapped and were held together with string or wire.

I was not there long when Patsie Foley came by and asked me if I would like to go for a boat ride. It was my first time in a boat. Patsie had a set up for pike fishing: it was a long line with a type of float on the end, and every few feet as it drifted away he would attach a drop line with a hook and bait on it. He caught a few pike before we came back. There were no life jackets in the boat but we made it back okay.

When I got back to my fishing rod it was still anchored where I left it. I pulled the line in and there was a good size pike on it. As I pulled the hook out of his mouth there was a small perch on the hook. The little perch got swallowed by the pike. That was one of my better Sunday's fishing.

There was a small wooden church in Fahy. Some evidence of its existence is in the Larkin map of 1818. The old church in Ballinaglera was located in Mulvey's yard. It was a thatched building.

The present Ballinaglera church (St. Hugh's) was completed in 1842. In 1938 there was a new roof put on the church. I remember one time standing in water in the back half of the church holding my father's hand. Father Dolan was the priest then. In addition to the roof, Father Dolan replaced the wooden alter with one made of marble. He also changed the location of the entrance gate up to the front of the church. Our schoolteacher, Gerald Kellegher, was the organist in the church choir. The choir was located inside the front door on the left with a few steps leading to it, sort of a loft.

Main Street
Dowra
Early 1900s

Main Street
Dowra
2005

Aerial view
Ballinaglera
Date unknown

6

Life in Dowra and Derrinageer

୫◇୫

Fair Day, the Farm, Moin Rua, and Mattis Hollow

The fair (market) day in Dowra was the third day of every month unless the third was on a Sunday, then the fair would be held on Monday. On these days the road was busy with cattle and sheep on the way to town. Some of the farmers that had enough land to feed a horse went to town in the trap, or sidecar, pulled by their horse.

The fair day was a great day with a lot of excitement, at least that's the way I saw it as a kid. The people came from all of the surrounding parishes so there were always a lot of people there. The farmers that had cattle or sheep for sale were there early in the morning.

Sometimes the buyers, or jobbers as they were called, would meet the farmers outside of town and make them an offer for their cattle or sheep before the farmers even got to the market. In town, the farmers brought the animals they wanted to sell to an area that was called "the Green." There was nothing green about it. It was on the side of a hill with no grass on it behind the main street in Dowra.

In the 1940s, the Garda (police) were stationed in Dowra and they rode bicycles; if one went past on the Loughy road it would be the news of the day. The only automobile in the whole parish of Ballinaglera belonged to Francy Lee. He used to drive the Clancys (Peter and our teacher Eileen) to Mass every Sunday. If another car went up the Loughy Road it would be the talk of the town land. Today most of the people who live in Ballinaglera have cars. The tractor has replaced the horse. The cattle and sheep are taken to the fair by truck.

Our farm is at the highest point on the Loughy road as it levels off and before it goes downhill. We had an iron gate at the entrance to our property at the road with a stone-built post on each side. The posts were about three feet square. When I was a young lad, I would climb up the gate, stand on the top rail, and walk across the gate to the other side, and jump off. On the side of the gate there was a stone ditch (fence). This ditch had a stile built into it. The stile was steps up one side of the ditch and down the other. If you were coming down to our house you could go over the stile rather than opening and closing the gate.

When I was living there, the fields by the road were pasture where the cattle and donkey grazed. Some years later my brother Bernard changed them to meadows. The two fields at the bottom of our land, which were the meadows in my time, were made into pastureland. I think the reason for this change was access to water for the cattle if the summer got hot, and there was a chance of the well running dry. I mentioned a few pages back that at the bottom field of our land was a spring-fed stream. I think it was a good idea to change the use of these fields. We only had two fields along the road, but they were big fields. The road frontage was approximately two or three thousand yards.

Looking down from the road and on the left of our land is Patrick Gilrane's land. At the bottom of our land is Stephen Gilrane's. Coming up on the right is Owen Simpson's meadow. Above Owen's meadow Patrick Gilrane has two more fields that go up to the road. Owen Simpson did not live close to us, and I often wonder how he got this one meadow next to our land. Owen was an old man when I knew him. He always wore burlap leggings winter and summer.

Owen was not the only one that had odd fields that were not next to their main farm. We had two fields that were not near our land. One field we called "Moin Rua," which is an Irish phrase that means "red turf," and how we got this field I do not know. Moin Rua was located at the back of the hill facing the mountain. It was in between Stephen Tammy's land and Terrie Foggie's. We kept this field as a meadow. It was not a big field, usually three cocks of hay.

To get to Moin Rua from our house, we went towards Dowra on the Loughy Road. Two fields down on the right we went through Stephen Tammy's pasture till we came to our Moin Rua, which had a fence (called a "ditch") with a "shough" for drainage around it. The fence was made of clay and stone and we had to make a gap in the ditch to get through it into our land. The water in the shough had a good flow and it was necessary to make a "kesch" in the shough. A "kesch" could be described as a miniature bridge. It was made from the stones that were available. When we were finished working in this field, and would not be back for a while, we would close the gap in the ditch with a whitethorn tree that we cut down. We would just place the whitethorn tree in the gap with a few stones on top to keep it in place.

I don't know how we got this field. It was less than an acre and not very good land. One year we planted potatoes in the whole field but the distance from the house made it impractical to use this field for potatoes every year. The cow manure that we used for fertilizer had to be taken there with the ass, and the potatoes had to be brought back in the creels on the ass. It was easier to use land closer to the house. The other years we just saved the hay from this field, although we only got three cocks of hay off of it.

There was another field called "Mattis Hollow." This field was quite a distance from the house. It was between Patrick James Peter Terry's and Stephen McGrail's land. Patrick told me a story that he heard when he was young as to how we got Mattis Hollow. We had two head of cattle that were grazing at the field and at that time there was a byre on the field. The man's name that owned it could have been Mattis. Well, it seems that he liked a little nip now and then and he also liked to smoke a few fags (cigarettes). The two head of our cattle were in the byre for the night and so was Mattis. During the night Mattis finished his bottle and a few fags, then the byre burned down and so did our two head of cattle. We were compensated for the loss of the cattle by getting the field. That's the story Patrick told me and from that day on it was known as "Mattis Hollow."

We used this field for hay; it was bigger than Moin Rua and a little better land. When the hay was saved and brought home, we would put some cattle there to eat the aftergrass. The ditch around this field is shaped like a capital "M". In one corner of the field there is a well. I think it is spring-fed (artisan). The Stephen McGrails used this well for water for the kitchen. When I was working in Mattis Hollow it was nice to see Bridie or Alice McGrail come to the well for a bucket of water. As a young fellow we had great imaginations.

To bring the cattle to Mattis Hollow we had to go through a few fields of Patrick Gilrane's. This meant making a gap in the ditch to Patrick's land and a gap into Mattis Hollow. These gaps had to be closed up after we were finished.

Looking back on these two fields I think they were a waste of time because they were so far from our house, but when I was very young I loved to go with my father to work these fields.

The main farm by our house wasn't the best of land. The pastureland had a lot of rushes growing on it that grew to about two feet tall. They were not good for the cattle to eat, and the fields that had lots of rushes didn't have much grass. We always tried to keep the rushes cut but they grew like weeds. Sometimes they grew in bunches and we called this a "purtlouge" of rushes—a bunch of them growing together in a circle about 15 inches in diameter. We used the rushes for thatching the stacks of turf and also for thatching the hay and oats after they were brought in to the haggard for the winter. Another use for the rushes was thatching the hen house and the byre where we kept the pig. They were not as good a thatch as straw but they would last a year or more.

In the meadows where the hay was cut every year there were no rushes so it would seem they could not survive a yearly cutting. When we gathered the hay, we stacked it in the lower haggard.

We brought the cocks of hay in from the meadows and made one big stack that was called a "pike." The base of this pike was about 15 or 20 feet wide and could be as high as 25 or 30 feet and came to a point on the top. This pike of hay was then thatched with rushes and tied down with ropes that were spun from the hay. The oats were also brought in to this haggard and made into large stacks. It was also thatched with rushes and tied down. We had a very small field on the upper side of the house that we called the "upper haggard." We made a stack of the turf in this haggard and they were also thatched with rushes. As I mentioned, the rushes were not good fodder for the cattle but we used a lot of them for the thatch.

Around the house and the byre and barn, and not too far from the old dung hill, grew the nettles and dockins. The nettles were about 12 inches tall and if you brushed against them they would sting and cause a mild rash. There was a good cure for this nettle sting. By taking the stalk of the dockin and skinning it you would find clear slimy fluid. This dockin extract would cool the nettle sting and keep it from becoming a rash. The cattle would not eat the nettles or the dockins. Today in health food stores they sell "stinging nettle root." If we only knew. The dockins and the nettles did not spread through the fields like the rushes.

Another plant that grew in the pasture was the "buchallan." This plant grew to about two feet tall with a yellow flower. It looked like the dandelion but much taller. The cattle would not eat them so we used to pull them out roots and all. Also in the pasture grew the thistles. They were not easy to pull or get a hold of because they were covered with stickers. Now with the rushes, the dockins, the nettles, the buchallans, and the thistles there was plenty of weeding to be done.

The Sisters,
Mary Edwin &
Theresa Agnes
with my
Grandmother,
Mary Fitzpatrick

Urbal National School
& Outhouse

7

The Family

❦

The Urbal National School

Now back to my early years in the old homestead.

As I mentioned earlier, my mother died before I was a year old. I do not remember her at all as there were no pictures taken when they were married or of their years growing up. I do remember my grandmother Mary, but not that much about the day-to-day routine of the house. I remember she made a small cake for my lunch on my first day of school. School lunch was usually a slice of buttered homemade bread with a bottle of milk. That was a special lunch, a piece of cake with the milk. I remember her getting ready for church on Sundays with her bonnet that had ribbons tied under her chin. She would walk to church through the fields. All of the ditches had stiles so they were no problem. As she went past Mary Ann James Peter, she would wait for her and further on they would meet Bridget McGrail. Husbands and wives did not go to church together. They went through the fields, met their friends, and walked together. In the Ballinaglera church, the men sat on the right hand side and the women on the left. Even today the seating is the same.

My grandmother Mary must have been a great help to my father. Bernard and Teresa were four years old and I was just one when our mother died. Sister Teresa and Sister Mary Edwin were home for a visit once but I do not remember them. Sister Teresa later told me when they were there they took my grandmother on a day trip and when they came back she said she wouldn't leave me again no matter what the sisters said.

I do not remember Grandma being sick but I came home from school one day and my father told me that Grandma had died. There were a lot of the neighbors in and out of the house. I did not know what a sad and lonely day this was because I was too young to understand. There were no undertakers in those days. The neighboring women came in and took care of grandma. John Rynn's store had all the funeral supplies.

Men and women were dressed for burial in what was called a "habit," a large, brown dress-like gown with scapular imprints front and back. The wake was in the house and lasted all night. My father said I could stay up all night and I remember falling asleep in the kitchen.

The afternoon of the second day Grandma was taken to church where she spent the night. On the third day was Mass and the funeral at Fahy graveyard. For my father, this was a sad day and I am sure a day of concern towards the future. He not only lost his mother, he had also lost a great helper.

When the funeral mass was over, it was customary that a collection be taken up, so a table was placed inside the alter rail. The priest and members of the family stood by the table while someone who could write quickly sat at the table and made a list of the donations. The people at the mass then came up and put some money on the table, usually a few shillings. The family members were usually first, followed by the men on the right side of the church, then the women from the left side. This obligated my father to do the same thing when there would be a funeral for any member of the families that came to his mother's. The money collected was for the priest.

When we left the church, John Rynn was waiting outside with the hearse. It was black with glass windows all around and was drawn by two black horses. The priest drove on ahead to be the first at the cemetery. Everyone else walked behind the hearse to the cemetery. If someone was out walking and they approached the funeral procession, they would join it and walk a short distance with the procession as a sign of respect, then they would turn off and be on their own way again.

When we got to Fahy, the grave was already dug. The clay was piled around the grave and was not covered with green cloth as it is in the States today. The priest would already be there and a few prayers would be offered before the casket was lowered into the ground. The priest would put the first shovel full of clay on top of the casket, and then the men who had dug the grave would fill it in.

It was not uncommon to have skulls and other bones from previous burials be dug up when the grave was opened. These were placed around the new coffin. After the grave was filled in, everyone went back to Rynn's for a pint.

When we talk about beautiful Ireland, Ballinaglera, Derrinageer, and all the lovely green fields, the lakes and the mountains, we get a very lovely and tranquil picture. With no modern conveniences in the home, life was not always easy. Now that I was old enough to be going to school each day with Bernie and Teresa, it was a little easier for my father since we were out of the house most of the day. After a breakfast of oatmeal, we were off to school with the standard lunch of bread and milk.

Our teachers were Miss Clancy and Mr. Gerald Kellegher. The men teachers were addressed as "master" and the ladies as "Miss." The school I went to was Urbal National School. It was built in 1890 and closed in 1975. It was a two-room school with about five long seats or benches in each room. Miss Clancy taught grades one through four, four grades and five benches, in the room on the right hand side. It had its own entrance. Master Kellegher had the room on the left where he taught grades five through eight. The same set up: four grades and five benches.

Each room had an entrance hall where coats could be hung up, and in the rear of the hall was a turf bin. It was also used to store coal and kindling. Each family with children in the school brought a load of turf to school for the winter. A load of turf was two creels full, which were carried to the school on the back of the ass.

Master Kellegher's desk was directly in front of the fireplace. On the left side of the desk was a large closet with shelves. The Master would take the roll call every morning and enter it in a large, green book. This book was at least three feet long and there were a lot of them there. They must have held entries that went back to the 1890s.

If you were in school early, the Master might ask you to sweep the floor. The floors were made of wood and were dusty. It was customary to sprinkle the floor with water to keep the dust down before sweeping. Another early morning chore was to make the fire or fill the inkwells. On each bench there was a row of holes that the inkwells fit into. The ink came in powder form. We had a large bottle where water was added to the powder. It was then shaken up and the inkwells were filled. These were some of the jobs you might do if you got to school early. If, on the other hand, you got to school late, you might meet the Master or Miss Clancy at the door with a stick in their hand. They would have you hold out your hand, palm up. That old stick sure did smart, especially on a cold morning. If Master Kellegher really got mad, he would hit you with the stick on the back of your legs. The black and blue welts from that one could last for days.

The right side of the schoolyard was the girls' side and the left was for the boys. There was a high wall separating them in the back of the schoolyard that went right up to the outhouse. The wall also separated the boys' and girls' sides of the outhouse. Every few years they had men come in. They would dig holes, clean out the pits and bury it.

Master Kellegher smoked cigarettes and when he finished with one, he would throw the butt outside. Sometimes these butts were a good length, almost half a cigarette, and they were in great demand. When he wasn't looking, we would pick them up, put the light out and smoke them later on when it was safe.

The lunchtime was a half hour and was spent outside playing. When the weather got warm in April or May, we went to school barefooted. The only time that we wore shoes after that was to church on Sundays. Going to school bare-footed was all right until you stubbed your toe on a stone. With a piece of skin off the toe and it bleeding, there was no turning back, just hop along. Old Master Kellegher did not have a first aid kit, so we had to wait until it dried up and stopped bleeding.

I believe that school closed for the summer at the end of May. This was a great day. Everyone was happy, even the teachers. My father liked to have us home because it was less work for him. It seemed like the summer lasted forever and we loved it.

Miss Clancy lived close enough to the school that she walked back and forth each day. Master Kellegher, on the other hand, had much farther to travel. The bicycle was the main means of travel them days and not all houses had one. When the master got to school, the bicycle was taken up the steps and into the classroom. In the spring and fall the master would, on occasions, walk through the fields to get to school, but it was a long walk.

I remember one time in the summer, when the girls were going to school, they took the long blades of grass in the meadows and made knots of them across the path. The girls were Bridie and Alice McGrail, Bridget Trush, and Teresa. It was a rainy morning and as the master was on his way, he tripped over the tied grass and fell down. The master was so mad that he punished the girls by making them kneel in the classroom.

The one thing that came to our attention was that Miss Clancy never went to the outhouse during the school day. Well, the old bucket that we wet the floor down, before it was swept, was in the back room. It probably never happened, but we thought that Miss Clancy pissed in that old bucket during the day.

In them days there were five schools in Ballinaglera, and all children walked to school no matter how far it was. Today there is one school in the whole parish. There are a lot fewer children in the parish, and now they have school buses. There are vocational schools in Drumkeerin and some of the children are bused there. Times have changed.

When you reached 14 years and completed the eight grades, that was the end of school. It was a great feeling to be finished with school. Fourteen years old and out of school, I considered myself a man. I was wearing long pants. Life was great.

Our upper field

The path down to our byre & house

The gate where I said my goodbyes in 1947

The byre that still stands, thanks to a metal roof

8

The Farm in Spring

❧

Putting in the Crops; John Frank Tammy; and The Turf

Springtime on the farm was a busy season. If it wasn't raining most of the time, it would have been easier. The field where the potatoes were last year would be the first to be dug (turned over). This was done with the "loy." The loy was made of wood. On the end of the loy, the part that goes in the ground, there was an iron tip that was about four inches wide. It was a long stick with a notch on the side just about a foot before the end of it. This notch came in handy when we had to press the loy into the ground with our foot. The loy weighed between five to ten pounds and digging with it was not easy work.

Martin Wiley McTiernan was a great carpenter. He made the loy for my father. Martin could make the loy for a right or left handed person by placing the step on either side of the shaft. The tip was made in the forge by Myles Flynn. Myles and his brother Bernard were blacksmiths. They made everything by hand in the old forge. It was tempered by the blacksmith and sharpened

When this field was dug we planted oats in it. The seed oats were sprinkled around by hand. Next we went over the area with a "graip" or a shovel to loosen the ground and try to cover the seeds. A "graip" is a short handled tool with four prongs that are about ten inches long. The graip has many uses on the farm. On a few occasions we borrowed Hubert Ford's horse and harrow. This was the easy way to plant oat seeds.

To plant the potatoes was a lot more work. If you were planting them in a pasture field that had a lot of rushes, it was not easy to make the ridges. The rushes had a mesh-type of roots that were hard to turn over. The first step in making the ridges was to score a line with the loy. We used what was called a "scoring rope," a long rope that would go from one side of the field to the other. We had two sticks about three feet long attached to each end of the rope. With these sticks we measured off the width of each ridge where the potatoes were to be planted. When the whole area was scored off in three feet sections, we went to the next step.

The next job was to bring the cow manure from the dung pile and spread a row of it between the scored area. This was done with the old ass and a square wooden box on each side. We called them "pardoges." The pardoges had a trap door on each one. We would lead the ass to the dung pile, fill up the pardoges, and then drive the donkey to the field. We would lead him in between the scored area then pull the rope off the stick that kept the trap doors closed. It was then spread out between the scored area and a sod was turned over on each side making the ridge where the potatoes were planted. It could take days to put out the manure this way.

The loy was used to turn the sods over, and some loose earth was used to close any area between the sods. When the whole field was made into ridges, the next step was to plant the seed potatoes. We used small potatoes from last years' crop for seed. If there were not enough small potatoes, the women would take big potatoes and cut a section out that had an eye. Sometimes you could get more than one seed from a big potato. The last step was to put the seed in the ridges. This was done with what we called a "stievene." The stievene was a long piece of wood that came to a point. About six inches before the point it had a peg sticking out on one side. Sometimes the women would use the stievene and make holes in the ridges by stepping on the peg.

My job when I was small was to drop a seed in each hole. They called this "guggering." The holes would be closed by hitting the side with the stievene or the graip. I remember one time when I was a small boy, I spent the day guggering for Patrick and Linnen.

Our closest neighbors

Patrick & Linnen Gilrane
and their home

She was making the holes with the stievene and I had the bucket of seed potatoes, dropping one in each hole as Linnen made them. James and Maryann, Patrick's father and mother, were living then. At dinner that day when we finished, they had turnips and potatoes. Maryann was a very forceful woman (bossy). The turnips that were not eaten by the others got piled on my plate with the old standard, "eat them all up now. They are good for you." That night I was sick to my stomach. The next time Patrick and Linnen wanted me guggering for the day, I was hiding under the bed.

Planting potatoes and sowing the oats could take weeks depending on the weather. We got a lot of rain and some days we worked rain or shine. With the potatoes, the oats, and the cabbage planted there was some time with not too much to do. The meadows where the cattle could graze all winter would be closed off in the spring so that they hay could grow.

The pig was also bought in the spring at the fair in Dowra. It was always a small one that my father would bring home in a burlap bag. The pig was always let out in the pasture where it would live. It always had two rings put in its' nose to keep it from digging holes in the pasture. If it was a male, it would also get castrated. Terry Gilrane was always called on to perform both "operations". The pig was fattened all year and near the end of October or beginning of November we had the pig butchered (Terry took care of this, too). This was always a sad day in a way. The pig had become very friendly and loved to be rubbed. If you started rubbing him, he would lay down in front of you so that you could rub his belly.

After the pig was butchered, the pig was boned out. There would be six parts of the meat: the two front quarters, the two rear quarters, and two from the center. The six pieces were salted and placed in a wooden box. After three weeks in the salt, the bacon was cured and was then hung in the corner of the kitchen because it did not need to be refrigerated. It was good bacon but always tasted salty.

The women were great at making the bread. They did not use a recipe. The flour was bought at Rynn's store and was sold by the stone (14 pounds). Two of the name brands that I remember were Millacrat and Pride of the West. The flour came in a white cloth bag. It was not unusual in school to see a girl with an undershirt that said "Pride of the West" on it. The bread was baked in the oven that hung over the fire. There was a lid placed on the oven and coals from the fire were put on top of the lid while the bread baked. A slice of hot bread and butter with a mug of buttermilk always hit the spot.

The next work to be done at the end of May was cutting the turf. I always liked going to the mountain to work on the turf, even though it was a long walk. It took one hour to get all the way to our turf banks. Sometimes we took the ass up with us and brought back a load of turf. It was too far to come back for lunch so we brought some buttered bread and some tea with us.

All of the turf banks were over the top of the mountain. Going up to the mountain and after passing the old stone wall which was the end of private land, it became very a steep climb. At the top there was a flat area that was called "the play bank" where most people had their banks. I never saw anyone playing there, and I don't know how it got the name. From there it went down to a valley. There were a lot of turf banks there. On the other side of the valley was another raised area and past that were more turf banks. The other side of the mountain if you kept going was Glengevlin, Co. Cavan.

A turf bank could be six sods deep, or even more. The turf was cut with a spade that had an extended wing on one side. We would press the spade into the ground as far as it could go, cutting the turf into lengths about the size of large bricks, about three inches square and a foot long. The metal part at the end of the turf spade is about a foot long and that is as far as it is inserted into the turf bank. There is a blade on the side of the spade which can be on either side much like the step on the loy, if you are right handed or left. After they were cut we would spread them out to dry on the heather or wild grass that grew there. When the sods were partially dry we made "futtings" of them. A futting is about six to eight sods stacked in an upright position like a teepee. They dried faster in futtings because of better air movement around the sods.

The last step when they were dry was to make a stack of them. We made our stack about a quarter mile from the banks and always in the same place. It would have been faster and easier to make the stack on the banks where they were cut, but stacking them where we did made it much easier when we went to bring them home. This way, we didn't have to go over the top of the mountain when we came back to haul them home.

To make this stack could take a few days. There was only one way to bring them to the stack and that was with the ass and creels. We had only one ass but for stacking the turf we would borrow extra asses from the neighbors. With three or four asses and some help filling the creels, the stacking of the turf went fast. It was hard work because you were walking all day and bending over picking the turf up to put in the creels. When the stack was finished and all the turf in from the banks, we would thatch the stack with rushes and tie the thatch down with ropes. The cutting and saving the turf went okay if the weather was good. We did not always get good weather and the rain made it seem like they would never dry.

The mountain was very high and if the day was cloudy there would be a mist that kept everything wet and damp. Not good for drying turf. I remember days when it got misty and started to rain. Not far from our banks on the other side of the mountain there was a very large slab of rock that stuck out. Underneath this rock was an opening the size of a large room. When the rain started we took shelter under this big slab of rock. Sometimes we made a fire and heated our tea. If the rain did not stop we had to leave for home and by the time we got there, we were wet to the skin. You get used to being wet and cold on the bogs.

One time my brother Bernard and myself were cutting turf on this bank and Mrs. McPartlin came by. I don't remember her first name. She was Sweedin's mother. Anyway, she said that the bank we were cutting was hers. There were some heated words between her and Bernie. But he kept cutting and throwing the sods out on the bank as far as he could. As she was moving around and giving us a piece of her mind, she got hit with a wet sod of turf in the chest. Well, she had Taylor McHugh write a nasty and threatening letter to our father. As best I remember nothing came of it, and to this day I don't know whose bank it is.

When the weather was good it was fun, saving the turf. There were a lot of people going up to the mountain. If there were more than one girl in the family, they went and helped. Coming home in the evening was easier than going up, because it was all downhill. It was also a time to talk with the neighbors. Now if you brought the ass and creels with you in the morning, then you had to come down the old road. The old road started at Myles Darcy's dipping tank and ended at the Loughy Road. It was not fenced in like most roads, so as you were leaving Myles Darcy's land you would have to open a gate and close it behind you. It then went through John McGuire's land and then on through John Frank Tammy's land. There were a total of three gates to be opened and closed.

Just a few words about John Frank Tammy. John's house was on the road to the mountain. He had a small farm of land and lived by himself. Old John had very bad eyesight, yet he had done some work on his small farm. He had only one cow and a young calf, a donkey and some chickens at one time. As the years went by, his eyesight got worse.

It was a long walk from his place to our house, but John would come rambling some times at night. He would carry an old lantern all the way and not miss our gate to turn off. John smoked the pipe, and he was a sloppy smoker. When he went to spit out, most of the time he missed the floor and he would end up spitting on the side of the old overcoat he was wearing. It was easy to tell when John shaved because his face was only clean where the razor had traveled.

The winter that John died, I was working on the road that went by his house to the mountain with Jimmy Paddie and Myles Darcy as the ganger (boss). It was getting late in the day and there was no smoke coming from John's chimney. Myles got concerned and said we should check to make sure John was all right. As we opened the door to his kitchen, the chickens that he had came flying out. We went to the upper room where we found John lying in his bed. He was dead and had been for some time as he was stiff as a board. Because of the condition of his house, there was no wake that night. Instead, John was taken to the church. John Gilmartin took over the funeral arrangements. Since John Frank Tammy didn't have any family, the foresters took over his land some years ago and planted it all over with pine trees. There is not a trace of his house or byre today and not many people remember John. He is buried in Fahy in an unmarked grave. He was a nice old man who had a hard life.

After we got home from cutting or bringing in the turf and had our dinner, it was off to Dowra or down to John Rynn's store. There wasn't much to do in either place. Cigarettes were called "fags" and a five cigarette pack was called a single Woodbine. That was the brand name and it cost three cents in them days. During World War II, cigarettes were scarce. When John Rynn waited on us very young smokers, we would be lucky to get a single woodbine. The older men got a double Woodbine. Sometimes John would have a large box of cigarettes loose. We usually only got three cigarettes.

After we got our fags, we would sit outside on the wall and talk for a while. Sometimes a girl would walk by. By ten or eleven o'clock we were heading home. That was too late to go rambling. The summer months were not as good for rambling because the nights were too short.

Later on in the fall we would bring the stack of turf home and rebuild the stack in the upper haggard. It could take days to bring them home. If you could borrow five or six extra asses and have someone help you, it went pretty fast. It was a great feeling to have a good stack of turf in the upper haggard. You knew you were all set for the winter.

Typical Kitchen in
Irish farm cottage

Butter
Churn

Turf sods
stacked for
drying

Spade used
to cut turf
by hand

Turf sods
in creels
for transport
home on
donkeys

9

Summer and Fall

❧

Bringing in the Hay, Turf, and Potatoes

By the end of July and beginning of August it was hay time. If the weather was good for a few weeks, it would be saved. Some years when we had a lot of rain it dragged on and on. There were no cattle grazing in the meadows since the beginning of May, so the hay was tall. We did not have a horse and machine to cut our hay, so we cut our fields with the scythe, which made it very hard, work. The hay was cut in a straight line about 50 feet. This was called a "swart." When you got to the end of the swart, you walked back and started another one.

There were no weather reports but the old folks could tell what the outlook was for the next few days. Their forecast was based on a few things: the wind direction, the cloud formation, the reflection in Lough Allen of the clouds and their formation, and the way the crows and swallows were acting. If the forecast was not good, you would not cut much hay.

After you had a field of hay cut down, the swarts had to be shaken out or spread evenly on the ground. With a little luck from the weather, in a day or two you could make "cocks" of the dry hay. A cock of hay was a large round heap that came to a point at the top. The sides were combed down with the rake so all the blades of hay were pointing downward. This way the rain would run off it much the same as the thatch on the house.

If the weather became wet, or as we used to say "showery," we would make "laps" of the hay. This was done by raking the hay into a roll, then starting at one end we would shake the hay into a small pile. We would then pick up the pile, tuck in the outside edges and then place it back on the ground. The rain would roll off the top of the "laps" so most of it would stay dry. If the next day was sunny, we would shake out the laps. When it dried, we would pile it up into cocks.

At the end of August or the beginning of September the cocks of hay would be brought in and a "pike" or "rick" would be made from it. A pike was the same style as the cocks only ten times larger. The rick was a long pile of hay coming to a head. The shape resembled the thatched cottage. The cock or rick would be thatched with rushes and tied down with ropes. It was called "putting in the hay" and when I was young it was a lot of fun. Since putting in the hay was a big job and had to be finished in one day because of the chance of rain, all of the neighbors would get together and put the hay in for one family. So there were many days spent putting in the hay. Again, there were no tractors or horses. We used the ass.

When the day came to put our hay in, the neighbors came and they brought their donkeys and ropes to help us "tress" the hay. Two ropes were placed by the cock of hay in the field, the hay was rolled on to the ropes, and tied into a "rool." Then the rool would be placed on end, the ass would be brought alongside it and the rool would be placed on his back. One man would walk behind the ass and balance the rool as the ass carried it to the haggard. There would be three or four men in the haggard making the pike, or rick. So we had two crews of men: the haggard crew and the men that were bringing the hay in on the asses.

As a kid it was a fun day. I might have to rake up some hay that fell off the tresses or help spin a rope to tie it down. The ropes were made from hay. We used a twister that was made from an old bucket handle. One man would spin the rope and I would twist it. It was similar to the old spinning wheel but not as modern.

When the day was over and all the hay in, thatched, and roped down, we had dinner. This was the best part of the whole day. Dinner in each house was usually the same: potatoes, cabbage, and bacon. The cabbage was chopped up after it was boiled. It was then simmered in the bacon fat, plenty of salty bacon fat. Boy, was it good.

It was a great day and everyone was happy to get the hay in the haggard before the weather got bad. The stacks of oats were also brought in to the haggard and thatched with rushes and roped down. Bringing in the oats was not as big a job as the hay. Each household brought in their own oats.

After we brought in the oats to the haggard and stacked them, we would separate the grain from the straw. In order to do that, we had to take the straw into the barn. We placed a wooden barrel on its side and then take a sheaf of oats (several handfuls tied together with some of the straw) and smack them against the side of the barrel. This would cause the grain to fall off the stalk and what was left was the straw.

After buffing the oats, the grain was put in burlap bags, and with the grain was the chaff, a light covering over each grain of oats. The next step was to separate the grain from the chaff. This was done on a windy day. A large cover was placed on the ground and the mixture of grain and chaff was placed in a sieve. As the mixture came through the sieve, the wind blew the chaff away and the oat grains fell onto the cover.

The oats were used mostly for feed for the chickens or some would be saved as seed for next year's planting. If we had too much, the excess could be sold. Making oatmeal for our breakfast out of our oats was something that was done in my father's day, not in mine. There wasn't a mill in operation in Ballinaglera when I was a boy, so we had to buy our oatmeal in Rynn's store.

The roof of the house had to be thatched every few years. Sometimes the rushes were sued for the thatch, but they were not the best and would not last long. The best thatch was the straw left over after separating the oat grains. The cattle would not eat the straw but it was great for thatching the house and would last a lot longer than the rushes.

If the weather was still good we always tried to bring the turf home. This could take a week or two. We only had one ass so when the time came to bring home the turf, we would borrow one from Patrick, Stephen Tammy, Tommy Terry, and anyone else that we could. Can you imagine going over to Patrick's in the morning and meeting his wife Linnen and asking her if we could borrow her ass for the day?

As the days got shorter in the fall, two trips were all you could make to the mountain each day to get the turf. If you had four or five asses, it went pretty fast. The creels were filled to the top, then sods were placed standing on end around the edge and then the center was filled in. It was a long walk up to the mountain, all up hill. If it started to rain on the way up, we kept going and completed the first trip. If the rain lasted, we would call off the second trip when we got home. We had lots of rainy days and some days were showery. This could stretch bringing turf home for weeks.

My father stacked them up as we brought them home. He was very good at it and real neat. All of the outside sods were sloped downward and were gradually stacked to a point. The stack was then thatched and roped down for the winter. The turf made a nice clean fire and the only expense was our time, which we had plenty of. The turf banks in the mountain were in our family for years.

Some years we did not have enough good weather to save the turf. This made for a long, cold winter. We had some trees that we cut down but it took a lot of wood to last the winter. The fire was hard to start in the mornings, and someone had to be in the house all the time to keep it going. The one winter I remember going to get some coal was my only trip to the coal mine (Poll Glas) in Slievenak-illa.

Coal is very heavy, almost as heavy as stones, so with only one donkey you could not put much coal in each of the creels. To make it worth the long trip, I had to get a few more asses. I went to Patrick's to borrow their ass for the day. Their old ass was out in the pasture somewhere so I had to find him and bring him back to get the creels and mats on his back. Then I went to Terrie's and borrowed theirs. The same thing happened there: go out to the fields and find him, bring him back, get the creels and mats on him and bring him to our house.

Now to find our ass and get him ready and I was ready to go. With three asses I could bring home enough coal to last for a while. It was a long walk up to Slievenakilla Mountain. I had to go out the Loughy Road to John Frandie's then on the Slievenakilla Road to Poll Glas. It was about a two-hour walk each way and it took the whole day.

On the way up I met old Willie Smullins. He had a few asses and he was on his way to get coal, too. Further on we met a young girl on her way to get a load of turf. She had one ass (to carry her turf). I don't remember her name. I remember Old Willie doing some bragging about how good he was at making the little black cat purr. Later on I think I knew what he meant but not on that day.

It was a long day. We finally got to Poll Glas and got the coal in the creels, but I don't remember how much I paid for it. The creels were not the best way for bringing the coal home because some small pieces would fall through the creel with the movement of the donkey. When I got home and unloaded, the asses were left on our land overnight, but the creels and mats were put in the barn.

Now we had to get the old wood fire burning, then put some coal on so at least half of the kitchen was warm. A turf fire was not necessarily a warmer fire, but it was certainly more convenient. A winter without turf was long and cold.

The straddles, mats, and creels were all handmade at home so there was no expense for these items. My father made the mats from straw. They were woven together and covered with burlap. The straddle was a V-shaped piece of a tree that was anchored to the mats. It had holes in both sides and pegs were inserted in them. The creels were made of sally rods and hung on each side of the donkey on the pegs. It worked and cost nothing for materials. So from the first day on the mountain cutting the turf to the last day bringing them home there was no out of pocket expense, and you had a year of fuel for heating and cooking.

The same was true for most of our food supply including the milk, butter, potatoes, vegetables, bacon, and eggs. Now with the hay and oats safely in the haggard and the turf stacked and thatched out back, all that was left was the digging of the potatoes.

This was a backbreaking job because you were bent over almost all of the time. Some years, when the weather in the fall was bad, digging the potatoes was the last big job before winter and might not get finished before November. The ridges were turned over with a graip or short-handled loy. We used buckets and creels to gather them. They were sorted as we picked them. The small ones we called "pogeens" and they went into a separate pile. They would be used next year for seed or would be cooked for the chickens and the pig. The bigger potatoes were piled up in the field where you dug them, and late in the evening we would cut some rushes with the scythe and thatch the pile. On top of those rushes we would shovel about six inches of dirt all around. From a distance it would look like a big, long mound of dirt. The rushes kept the potatoes dry and the dirt kept them from freezing in the winter. We planted a lot of potatoes. Digging them in the fall could take a few weeks. Some years, in the spring, we would sell what we did not need.

One year I was working with Patrick next door. His wife, Linnen, was also digging with us, and she was a great worker. I had trouble keeping up with her. When the three of us started in the morning, we each had our own ridge to dig. I had to work fast to keep up with Linnen. The best part of the whole day was supper when we finished. Patrick's mother, Mary Ann, was alive at the time and she did the cooking. Some nights we had chicken and dumplings. Boy, that was good. Patrick would give me a shilling or two for the day's work, which was worth about 30 cents. When the potatoes were all dug and stacked, we were ready for winter.

10

The Winter Work

❦

Pat and Bessie Kellegher, Maggie & Michael Flynn, and the Christmas Season

I always liked the winter months, especially when we were finished with school. When we were in school, it was the same old routine day after day. Rain or shine we went to school. When we were out of school, however, the winter was a great time. To start with, we got up later in the morning. The cattle had to be foddered, cows milked, and chickens fed, just the usual day-to-day stuff. Some days we would also mend some ditches or drain some fields if it rained, but then that would be it for the day.

When supper was over and all the chores were done, the men went out rambling or went over to John Rynn's store and stood around the bridge by Gilday's house. If we had any money, we would buy a double of Woodbine for six pence. A bottle or pint of Guinness was a shilling. It was not often that we had enough money to buy a pint.

On the way home from Dowra, I often met Tommy Peter, or Patrick, or Francy Rynn. We would stand around the road to their house for a long time. Sometimes a few girls would walk by. Well, we would fall all over our shoes, and that's about all that would happen. After all this excitement, if it was early enough, we would stop at Myles Loughlin's house and ramble for a while. There was no hurry getting home. We were big, out of school 15-year-old men. It was good times then.

One summer during vacation from school I worked for James McTiernan (James Miley Andy). James was a building contractor and was away at work every day. They had three boys named JJ, Andy, and Oliver. (Oliver lives in the home now and is also a builder). The mother would make me a great breakfast of fried potatoes and eggs. I used to go to the mountain for a load of turf for them and work on their farm, helping with the hay and the oats.

I was about 15 when I started working for Pat Kellegher. His wife's name was Bessie. Pat and Bessie were an old couple. Pat walked with a limp and always carried a walking stick. Bessie walked a little bent over and had a cataract on one eye. They had an old dog named Captain and after a while, Captain would follow me everywhere. They had a small farm, a one-cow place. It started down by the road and went way up to the top of the hill. It was only one field wide and parts of the pasture were no more than 300-400 feet wide. Pat smoked a pipe and Bessie used snuff. When they ran out, I was sent to the store and Captain came along with me. I liked working for them. They did not pay much, but it didn't seem too important.

On the way there in the morning I went on the Loughy Road to John Gilmartin's. Kate Gilmartin would give me a wave from the window when I passed her house. I liked Kate. She was 19 or 20. Then I went through the fields past Andy McGrail's house, and the Kelleghers were the next place.

At the dances in the hall Kate wouldn't even give me a look because of the difference in our ages. She was a grown lady and I was just starting to shave. I used to go to her house rambling and if they wanted anything from the store, she would give me a wink or a smile and I would be off to the store rain or shine. Looking back now, they were fun times.

Pat and Bessie had one black cow and the McPartlin's next door also had one black cow. Well, the McPartlin's cow would cross over the old ditch and go up the Kellegher's hill. To get that thieving cow back where she belonged, I would send Captain up after her. That old faithful dog was up there in a flash and would know just which cow to send back over the ditch, then back down to the house he would come.

I helped Pat and Bessie with the hay, the crops, and cutting their turf. We got along great. All of their children were in America so there was no one else there to help them. One son, John, came home for a visit once, and he would be the one later on that helped me get to America.

I also used to help Maggie Flynn on her farm from time to time. I started helping her even before I finished school. Her husband had died, and she had one son named Michael who was a few years younger than I was. Maggie, as far as I remember, never paid me. I just helped out and got fed. She had a one-cow place and had some young cattle and a donkey. I used to go there at night rambling and sometimes I would fix Michael's shoes.

I got good at fixing shoes. At times I would rebuild the soles and heels. The old work shoes had a metal plate in the toe and rows of studded-type nails in the soles. These had to be replaced from time to time. The other shoes we had then did not have one piece for the upper part. The toe section came up to the bottom of the laces and the back part was sewed on to it on both sides. We called this seam the "yorkin" and the sewing had to be replaced as the shoes got older.

Maggie had a hard life after her husband died. She had to depend a lot on the neighbors. To make it even harder for her, all of her land was not in one parcel. Her pastureland was quite a distance from her house. It was a long walk to milk the cow in the summer. During the winter, the cow was kept in the byre by her house.

Maggie and Michael were known as the "sucks." The story as to how they got this name goes back to Maggie's mother-in-law. This was before my time, but the story goes that she was a large lady and a little rough around the edges. She was nicknamed the "Carrot." Well, the Carrot liked to brag as to how great she was on the farm and when she was working in the fields, she would tie her baby on to her back, throw one tit over her shoulder and let him suck. Well, the name "sucks" stuck.

During the winter months, we would drain some of the fields. The County Council had a program to help the farmers. They would tell us where to put the drains and how deep they had to be. They paid us some money for doing this work even though it was our own land. Some times during the winter, we would clean some shoughs along the road and fix up some ditches. The drainage ditch along the side of the road was called the "taoscadh" but we pronounced it "shough." Most winters weren't bad with snow but there were a lot of cold and rainy days. The winter seemed long, but when you are young time goes by much slower than when you are older. I always liked winter. The days were short without much work having to get done. The long nights were great for going out rambling.

The dances in the old hall were on Sunday night. They would not have them on Saturday because of Mass the next morning. We had to be awake for that one. The dances were fun. The hall was filled with young folks. There was one bench around the walls that was the only place to sit down. Before most dances were over there would be a fight, sometimes with 10 or 15 people involved. There was no telephone to call the Garda, and the closest police station was in Dowra. Most of the time there was just one man in the police station on duty so that by the time he rode his bicycle all the way to Ballinaglera hall, it would probably be the next day. Anyway, the fights were not that serious, just a bit of pushing and shoving, never any guns or knives. These fights usually started over a girl.

As the dance ended there was usually some pairing up for the trip home. There were no cars. If you were lucky enough to have a bicycle, and you were twice as lucky to have a girl to see home, she would sit on the handlebars of the bike and you peddled your brains out. When you took a girl home from the dance you would not be invited into her house for a cup of tea. It was not the custom. Now if the girl lived close to where you lived the trip wasn't bad, but if you had to go to the other end of Ballinaglera, it could take a few hours in each direction, but as the old saying goes, "It was just a hop and a skip there." It was the long walk back that hurt. On Monday morning, the gossip was getting started as to who was going with whom, and if there had been a fight, that would get center billing.

After I completed eighth grade, that was the end of school for me. Now my father had Bernard, Teresa, and me home all the time to help him so it got much easier for him. Teresa took care of the house and helped out on the land. Bernard used to help the neighbors on their farms in the busy seasons. The wages they were paid were very little, maybe one or two shillings a day.

The year before I left, Bernard was away in the bogs cutting and saving turf. That year I was doing most of the work at home. I dug and planted potatoes in the field by the road where our entrance gate is.

The Christmas season did not change much as we got older except that I did not go out with the wren like we did when we were younger. I did not mention going out with the wren before.

It was something that the young boys did on Saint Stephen's Day, that's the day after Christmas. We would get an empty matchbox, put it on top of a stick with a piece of holly sticking out of the top. I think the idea was that we had caught a wren and had him in the matchbox. We would then go to the neighbor's house and there was a little rhyme that we would say that went like this:

The wren the wren
The king of all birds
St. Stephens Day
He was caught in the furze.
Although he is small
His family is great.
Will your honor give

Us the price of a treat?
Up with the kettle
And down with the pan.
A penny or tupence,
To bury the wren.

People would give a penny or two, and that was a lot of money to me. Well, now we are older and can't go out with the wren. Christmas was a nice time but not like it is celebrated in the U.S. We did not have a Christmas tree. On Christmas night we would put a candle in each window and the front door was usually left open for anyone who might want to visit. We did not exchange presents and there were no toys for the kids. Money was always a problem.

On Christmas morning there was three Masses in the church and we stayed for all three. We left the house before it was light out. When we were small, we took the byre lamp with us and we left it at the gate in Mary Healey's meadow and picked it up on the way home. Riding the ass to John Rynn's to do the Christmas shopping was the best part of Christmas. The second best was getting up early on Christmas Day and going to mass in the dark with the old byre lamp.

When we came home, a special Christmas breakfast was fried Boxty with bacon that was just great. The night before Christmas, raw potatoes were grated and strained to a fairly dry consistency. Then they were mixed with flour and pressed into patties, which were then dropped into boiling water and cooked for some time. They were laid out to cool overnight. And Christmas morning, when we got back from Mass, the patties were split in two and fried in the bacon fat. They made a great breakfast on a cold Christmas morning.

One week after Christmas was "little Christmas," and on this night we went from house to house in a group. This was called "going out with the Mummers" and it was a custom that went back long before my time. When I was small, I remember a group of Mummers coming to the house. These were older men, some probably in their twenties. They had a musician that could play a fiddle or a flute, and they also had some men that could step dance so they put on a little show. They all wore some type of camouflage like a straw hat or a hat with a lot of ribbon streamers. They were always let in to every house and given a shilling or two.

The group that I went with was a watered-down version. We were just teenagers, no one could step dance, and I could not play any instrument, but it was fun going from house to house. A cold, rainy night did not help, but it did not stop us. We would try to get seven or eight people. The more the better. These were all boys. We liked to think of ourselves as men. The girls did not go. If we had ribbons we attached them to our hats or caps. They hung down covering our face. If we did not have ribbons, we made hats out of straw. These straw hats covered the whole head and face. To see, we looked between the blades of straw. We only wore these hats when we went in houses. They were supposed to be camouflage so people wouldn't recognize us. There was one man and he was the captain and the spokesman. Another of us would wear a straw "skirt" and that man would be "Mary Ann."

As we came to a farmhouse door, we put on our fancy hats. The captain announced (in a strange voice): "Here comes Captain Mummers and his daughter Mary Ann," as he knocked on the door. What we were supposed to do when they opened the door was that we all went into the kitchen to put on a show.

The times that I went out, we had no musician and we had no dancers, but that did not stop us. One time I was playing the harmonica. I stood outside the door because I didn't know one tune, but I made a lot of noise. The dancers inside were no better, just a lot of jumping around. Some houses gave us a shilling or two. They liked to see us come and of course it was the end of the Christmas season.

On a rainy night it was not as much fun. By the time we finished we were wet to the skin and our straw hat was like something you would find in the byre. The money that we got went to running a dance. Some of the dances we had were in private houses. It was not easy to find people who would let us have a dance inside their house.

One time we had a dance in Red Laughlin's house. It was on the hill just above Steven Tammy Tim's place. They were not living there at the time, which was good because we were having an all night dance. Another year we had a dance in Terry Win's. There was no one living there, either. Both of these houses have fallen down over the years. The music for the dance was from local players. We had great local players them days. Gerry Malvey was a great accordion player, Patrick Dolan played the fiddle, and Myles Laughlin played the flute. If we could get one or two of these guys we were all set. Sometimes a small collection was taken up and a keg of Guinness stout was brought in. The dance lasted all night.

Well this was the end of the Christmas fun and games. We still had the Sunday night dances and the rambling every night. There was no television, no electric or radio, but it was fun and most of all carefree times. When I look back on them days I wish I could turn back the clock. Ireland today is different. It is modern. Nothing in life stays the same.

After the beginning of the New Year time went by fast and by the end of February or the beginning of March we would start turning over (digging) the field where we dug the potatoes in the fall. This is the field where we would plant the oats this year.

I was still working for Pat and Bessie Kellegher. My brother Bernie would go up to the turf bogs in Athlone in another county. He would be there for a few months living in tents with other men cutting turf by hand for small wages. They call them now "Board a Moin" (Moin is an Irish word for turf). The turf these men cut was used to generate electricity and they built the power plants in the bogs. Over the years they have stopped cutting turf by hand; it is done now by large machines that top skim large areas.

The Loughy Road
& The Neighbors

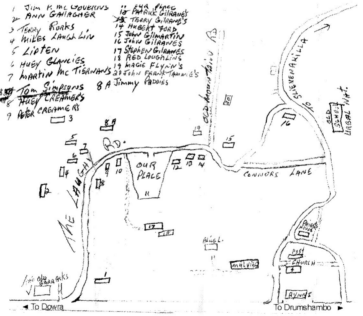

11

The Loughy Road & Our Neighbors

Our land is on the Loughy Road and I think it is the most scenic view in Ireland. As you stand at our gate by the road you can look to the west and see all of Lough Allen. On the far side of the lake is the town of Drumkeeran and the mountain range that goes all the way to Drumshambo. The large island in the lake is called "Inch Island." This island has the ruins of a church and also served the graveyard for Ballinaglera until the late 17th century.

It is a beautiful view. In the summer time, the people are out working the fields. Some areas are planted with potatoes, some with oats, and beautiful green meadows as far as you can see down to the lake. Looking in the other direction, to the east on the other side of the Loughy Road, you can see the high mountains. In the spring and summer the heather is in bloom with a bright purple flower. This is where we go each spring to cut the turf. Cattle graze part of the way up. This land is called the "tulaigh" and was owned by the farmers that lived close to the mountain. It was a continuation of their land. At the highest point of the tulaigh was a stone wall, which was the dividing line between the land that was owned, and the mountain. Sheep grazed on the higher areas and it was pretty in the summer. The view was breath taking.

This was the view from our gate, the best in Ireland and it still is.

The Loughy Road starts at the Old Barracks on the Dowra to Drumshambo Road about two miles south of Dowra. It is called the "Old Barracks" because at one time the police (Garda) were stationed there. From there the road is mostly uphill until you get to Jimmy Paddie's house, just before you would come to our property. From there it levels off until you pass Hubert Ford's, then it is mostly downhill to John Gilrane's house where it connects with the Slievenakilla Road.

Today there are not many families living along the Loughy Road. I remember the old days in the mid 1940s there were a lot of people living close to the road. Starting up from the Old Barracks the first house on the right hand side was Jim P. McGovers who married Bridget Darcy. Next on the left hand side was Ann Gallagher, who lived by herself in a small house that was one field from the road.

Next to Ann Gallagher on the left were Myles and Ann Loughlin who had no children. Some nights on the way home from Dowra, I would stop for a visit. This was called "rambling." Two fields above Myles and Ann's lived an old man we called "Lipton" who was rambling almost every night in Myles and Ann's.

Next house on the left was Ducky Clancy's place. "Ducky" was not her first name but that's the only name I knew her as. She lived with her father at the time. On the way home from dances in Dowra we used to go into their haggard and steal apples off their tree. By just shaking the bottom branches, a lot of apples would fall and we would fill our pockets. Well, when her father heard us he would come out yelling, chase us off, and set the dog after us. Ducky married a man by the name of Leonard, and his son is living in the place today.

The next house also on the left was Patrick McTiernan's (Patrick Martin Wiley). Pat, as he was known, had a lot of land. He had a horse at that time when most small farmers did not. A three-cow farm like ours was not big enough to feed a horse. It would have meant we had to get rid of two cows, that's how much the horse would eat. Pat used to take the milk to the creamery twice a week. He would start at his house on the Loughy Road and pick up cans of milk. From there he went to the Slievenakilla Road at John Frandie Gilrane's. From there to the Dowra Drumshambo Road at John Rynn's and on to the Dowra creamery. On the way back he dropped off the cans by the gate at the road and the cans had skim milk in them. Pat had a large family. Some of his children went to England and some to the States. Today his son Martin lives in the place, and his daughter Mary is married to John (Trush) Laughlin.

The next house on the right hand side was Tom Simpson's place. Tom was an old man as I remember him. I think he lived there by himself. Next house on the left was Jimmy and Bee McPartlin (Jimmy Paddy's). Jimmy and Bee had no children. Like most couples in Ballinaglera, Jimmy was much older than Bee. He passed away some years ago, and Bee died recently.

Next on the right was Huey Cremer. Huey was not married when I left in 1947 but he married some years later. I don't know his wife's name. Huey built a new house close to the road that his daughter lives in today. She is not married.

Next house on the right was Peter Cremer's (no relation to Huey as far as we knew). On Sunday mornings coming home from mass, Peter and my father would stand talking by the gate for an hour. All of the world's problems were discussed and solved. Peter had a large family. One son was a doctor, and another that they called "Sonny" stayed in the place and got married to Molly Mulvey. Sonny and Molly had children, but I don't know how many. Sonny has passed away and Molly is still living in the house.

Next on the right was our place, the "Tommy Dan Tim's." As I mentioned earlier, I was the fourth generation. Since my brother Bernard passed away in 1967, the house has not been lived in.

Our next-door neighbors were Patrick and Linnen. They had no family. When Patrick and Linnen got married, the old folks, that is Patrick's father and mother, James and Mary, were still living in the house. Linnen was a sister of Edmund Clark from Slievenakilla. I was very young when they got married. Linnen and Patrick have both passed away and today there is no one living in their house.

The next house along the Loughy Road on the right was Terry (Foggie) Gilrane's. Terry's wife's name was Kettie, and they had one son, Tommy, who married a girl named Bridget Wigger and they had two children, young Terry and his sister Mary.

There are a few things I remember about Old Terry. He always had trouble walking, and what I heard was that he had corns on his feet that were painful. One of his ways of starting a sentence was with the "Ah begarrah ..." saying. When it was time to kill the pig in the fall, Terry was always the man that we called.

I was very young, and it was always smart to stay out of Terry's way. I thought he was a bit cranky. There was one more job that we always called Terry for, and that was to castrate the male calves. We called it "cut the calves." This was done when they were a few months old. We kept the calf pinned against a wall until Terry was done. The calves just stood there so it mustn't have been too painful. There was never a charge for old Terry's services.

The next house was Hubert Ford's. Hubert was an old man as I remember him. Hubert's son, Garry, married John Gilrane's sister Rose. Garry and Rose had three girls and one boy. The Fords had a large farm of land, much bigger place than ours. They always had a horse and that was like having a tractor today. Some time after I left in 1947 the Fords sold their place to Tommy Terry Gilrane and moved to Co. Mayo. Now the Terry Gilranes have a big farm with both places.

As we go on the road from Fords, on the left was Maggie Flynn's. Maggie lost her husband and she lived with her son, Michael. Since then, Michael has moved to England and his mother Maggie has passed away. That house is empty now.

A little further down the road on the left is the road that goes up to the mountain, then on to John Gilmartin's, which is also on the left. John and his wife have moved to a senior citizen's home by the church. Their son lives in the old homestead and farms the land. After John's place you come to Connors Lane and on down the hill to John Frandie Gilrane's where it connects with the Slievenak-illa Road.

The Loughy Road was made in 1910. As far as I can tell there was no road there before then. It was not made for today's traffic. Some of the hills are steep even for the old horse and cart. It is very narrow with sharp bends. Two cars cannot pass each other on most parts. Sometimes cattle graze on the road, which creates a problem as they run in front of the car, or close to the side. Most times when I went to Dowra I would walk. To ride the bicycle was great going to town, all down hill. Coming back home was mostly walking, pushing the bike.

The fence on each side of the road (ditch) was a combination of piled up dirt with some stones mixed in. On some of these ditches, whitethorn trees were planted. The whitethorn was more of a bush. It had plenty of low branches and was a great windbreaker. In early spring it had beautiful white blossoms, then in the fall it had red berries that were edible called "sloes." As the lower branches of the whitethorn spread out, they made the road that much narrower.

Briars were plentiful along the road sometimes mixed in with the whitethorn. In the fall of the year, the briars were full of blackberries. They were better for eating than the sloes. Alongside the road is the ditch for drainage, which is called the "shough." From time to time the county council would have men working on the roads. Their jobs would be to clean out the shough and put the excess dirt that accumulated back on top of the ditch. This would keep the water flowing and not let it get out on the road. If the old whitethorn and the briars were out too far on the road, they would be trimmed back by the county men. Potholes would be filled with stones. Working for the county council on the roads was a good job in those days. The traffic on the Loughy Road was mostly walkers. It was a shortcut for the people of Slievenakilla going to Dowra.

12

A Death in Ballinaglera

❦

The Passing of Pat Kellegher

When I was 15 and 16 I did most of the spring digging and planting at home. I helped Pat and Bessie with their work as often as I could. With all of Pat and Bessie's children in America, it was very exciting for them to hear the news that one son, John, was planning a trip home. This was during World War II and John was in the service. Bessie always told me he was a "Corporal Commander and was over a group of men on the docks." She told me that a lot. The plans were that John would come home and then take his parents Pat and Bessie back to America. Well now the house had to be fixed up for John's homecoming.

Pat was on in years. I don't know how old he was but at the time I thought he was ancient. About this time Pat's foot started to bother him, and it was getting worse. He cut the top half off his shoe, which helped for a while, but it wasn't getting any better. It wasn't long till Pat was confined to bed and his second toe was black. Bessie made arrangements for the doctor to stop and see him. Well, the doc took one look and said it was gangrene and that it had gone too far. He said it was too late to consider amputation of the leg.

I don't remember how much longer he lasted. Bessie and myself were talking to him one afternoon and after a few deep breaths Pat was gone. This was the first time that I was present when someone died. It was the custom in Ireland at the time that when a person died suddenly it wasn't necessary to have a doctor pronounce them dead. Bessie and myself stood there watching poor old Pat as he turned pale. After a while, one of us closed his eyes.

When someone dies during the day, the wake is held that night. Bessie told me to go to John Rynn's store and get what we needed for the wake. John Rynn knew exactly what would be needed, and while he was getting it ready he gave me a pint of stout. Bessie also told me to stop at John Lackie's (Loughlin's) and have the bell at the church rung. When someone in the parish died they always rang the church bell for about a quarter of an hour slowly, with a pause after the third ring. This was a way of announcing throughout the parish that one of us was gone.

People were not buried in their regular clothes, so one of the items I brought back was the vestment the deceased wore. It was the same for men or women. They called it the "Habit." The wake lasted all night, so tobacco and fags (cigarettes) had to be supplied. During the night the women served tea and bread. The men sat around smoking and telling stories.

When I got back from John Rynn's some women had already come in to keep Bessie company. There were no undertakers so some of the men got Pat ready for his big night. He was dressed in his Habit and laid on the same bed where he died.

The next afternoon, John Rynn came with his horse-drawn hearse and he brought the coffin. Pat was placed in the coffin and carried by the men through the fields to the road. He spent the night in the church and the family attended mass in the morning. That afternoon, the funeral service was held at the church and from there we went to the Fahy graveyard. A few men went earlier and dug the grave. Everyone stayed until the grave was filled back up. The next stop was John Rynn's for a few pints. I went back with Bessie and spent a few nights sleeping at the house. It was sort of scary.

The fixing up of the house got started sometime after. There is not a lot you can do with the old three-room thatched houses. Tommy Terrie was a handyman and helped with some of the work. Most of the old farmhouses had a half loft in the kitchen. Well, Bessie had the loft extended the full length of the kitchen with a trap door for access. It looked better because now you could not see the old rafters. The house was whitewashed and some carpet runners were put on the floor by the bed. (The King is coming.) There still was no electricity and the bathroom was the closest bush or hedge. (When we had to go, we made it as quick as possible, especially on a cold rainy morning. Our toilet paper was always the same—a handful of grass or leaves. The chamber pot was strictly #1 (just like the bucket.) If you wanted water you went to the well or shough with the bucket. Not what a "Corporal Commander" was used to.

With my passport, a half empty suitcase
and a few dollars, I was on my way.

13

An Irish Son Emigrates to America

❧❧

Saying Good-bye to Ballinaglera

John came home and we got along well. He was a nice enough guy, but a bit more American than I was used to at the time. He dressed well; always a tie and collar, and he wore a wide-brimmed hat. I think the hat looked bigger because he was small.

We stopped a few times for a pint. He always bought because I had no money. John appreciated me working for Pat and Bessie and the many trips I made to John Rynn's store for tobacco for Pat or an ounce of snuff for Bessie. He was glad that I was around when his father died and that I stayed with old Bessie for a while after. John asked me if I would like to come to the States. Well, my answer was, "I sure would." John said that he would make out an affidavit of support, which was a guarantee that I would not be a burden to the United States till I became a citizen. If, for instance, I had no job and no money, the two people that made out the affidavits would have to support me. He also said he would stop and see my Aunt Catherine in Jersey City and see if she would be willing to help. Aunt Catherine was my father's sister, born and raised in the same old house as myself.

Before Bessie and John left, she sold everything she could in the old house. It must have been hard for her to sell off everything after spending all her life in the old place and raising a family there. Most of the stuff sold, even the rug runners that she bought to keep the Corporal Commander's feet warm as he stepped out of bed.

I was there the morning they left. When I look back now, it must have been sad for old Bessie. I stayed in the house till everyone picked up their stuff that they bought. Tommy Terrie bought the wood from the new loft and dismantled it after they left. I forget who bought the carpet runners, but everything went.

73

Well, that was the end of the Pat Stooks. I would not be passing by Gilmartins on the way there anymore and that would be less chance to see Kate.

The winter before I left I worked for the county council on the road and I was helping Maggie Flynn with some work. Her son Michael was a few years younger than I was.

I soon heard from John Kellegher and he sent me an affidavit of support. He had also gone to see my Aunt Catherine in Jersey City. She not only sent an affidavit of support but she also paid my passage. I don't remember how much it was, but it couldn't have been much. It was understood that I would pay it back when I started making the big bucks in America. So the wheels were in motion. It was just a matter of waiting for all the paperwork to go through.

There was a physical at the American Consulate in Dublin that I had to pass and I knew I had to have a tooth pulled before I could pass it. I borrowed my next-door-neighbor Patrick's bicycle for the trip to the dentist in Drumshambo. After that, I made the trip to Dublin by train from Carrick-on-Shannon and when I arrived, I passed the physical at the American Embassy. Things were falling into place.

When I got back home after my physical, Bernie gave me his old suitcase that he used when he had worked the bogs in Athlone. It was a big one, ten times too big for the few things that I had. I had a dress jacket that wasn't too bad. I think it was one of the pieces that I bought in Belcoo, Northern Ireland, and smuggled across the border when I went home. But I still needed a pair of pants.

I got a job with Tom Flood in Drumshambo. Tom had a bar on High Street as well as a small farm outside of town and that is where I would be working. He was also a tailor, and a good one, too. So for one week's work, Tom would make me a pair of pants to match my nice jacket. Tom had two sons about my age, Noel and Tom. It was a good week. Three good meals a day and the pants.

I got my passport and visa. The affidavits of support came and everything was ready. The sailing date was December 11, 1947. We did not have a farewell party. It was not the custom in Ireland them days. Some of the neighbors stopped in to say goodbye. Maggie Flynn, Michael's mother, stopped by. So did Mary and Bridget McTiernan. I don't think my cousin Mary Ann came but it is so long ago it is hard to remember.

My father got a car to take me to the railway station. It was the Convey's in Dowra that drove me to the train station in Carrick-on-Shannon. The only other car in Ballinaglera was Francey Lee's. I don't know why we did not get him.

I should have been sad that morning or even a little scared but I was young. I had no idea of what was ahead for me. My whole life up till now was the farm and the towns of Dowra and Drumshambo. I had never been to Carrick-on-Shannon. Teresa was home the morning when I was leaving. I said good-bye to her in the house.

My father, my brother Bernie, and myself headed up to our gate on the Loughy Road to meet the car, me with my big suitcase half empty. Patrick Gilrane stopped by before the car came. I remember Patrick saying, "We will all meet here at the gate again." As things worked out, that was not to be.

My father was sad to see me go, but he had to stay at the farm and work the day I left. Bernard made the trip to the train station in Carrick with me. This was the first time that I rode in a car. After saying my good-byes to Bernard, I took the train to Dublin and from there I got a train to Cork. I do not remember buying tickets for the train but I must have. I don't remember how much money I had. It could not have been much because I had no money of my own, and there was very little at home.

14

The Move to America

❦

Dependent on the Kindness of Strangers

I had booked passage on a ship that would leave from the port of Cobh, a few miles from the city of Cork. It was a whole day's train ride from Dublin to Cork and on the train I met an Irish-American man who was also heading for the States. I don't remember his name now, but it was reassuring to travel with someone that knew where we were going. We got off the train in Cork. I thought we were in Cobh because that is where I was to get the boat. Well, there was no other train going to Cobh that night so myself and this other man stayed in a hotel in Cork. The hotel was full, so I spent the night in a chair in the lobby.

The next morning it was a short ride to Cobh. I remember Cobh as being a lovely town on the ocean. It was a hilly town and there was a big church with bells that chimed. I had to check in at the ship's office. The ship I was to come over on was a converted troop transport called "The Marine Falcon" and it could not come in to Cobh because the water in the port was not deep enough. We had to take a smaller boat called a "tender" out to the big ship. The tender was like a ferry.

There were a lot of people saying their good byes, some crying and saying, "Come home soon." I still remember how the water looked so green. It seemed like it was a long trip out to the big ship.

I could not get over the size of the ship. The "tender" came alongside and we walked across a gangplank. The sleeping quarters on "The Marine Falcon" were double-decker bunks bolted to the floor and there were rows of them. I remember having a hard time finding my bunk but I finally did find it and got settled down. That same night after the tender left, we got underway. You could tell by the gentle rocking of the ship.

I remember breakfast in the morning. It was a table full of hungry young Irish. I don't remember what we had to eat but it had to be better than cold oatmeal. We had to be careful walking on deck as the ship was rocking from side to side and bobbing from back to front at the same time. Some people were seasick right from the start. I was lucky. I never got seasick and I did not miss a meal.

After a day or two the weather got very bad and the ship was getting tossed like a matchbox. A lot of people got hurt, some with broken bones from falling down stairs.

We had to keep our baggage under the bunk and the boat rocked so bad that my bag went sliding across the floor to the other side. No one was allowed on deck. You could have been swept overboard. The storm got so bad that at times they said we were not moving, and they had to go off course and steer the ship into the storm.

It took ten days till we saw the lights of New York harbor. I could not believe all of the lights. That night the ship stayed in the harbor and we came in the next morning, December 21, 1947. I don't remember much about getting off the ship but once we were off I had to hold on to things to steady myself as I walked—that was from ten days of rocking on the ship.

I had never met my Aunt Catherine or her husband Lester but I did recognize John Kellegher. They were all there to meet me along with my cousin, Catherine and Lester's only son, young Lester, and they took me to their apartment at 144 Duncan Avenue in Jersey City, New Jersey. It was a cold water flat, called so because there was no heat. They were "railroad rooms" which were a series of rooms with no doors on any of them. My Aunt Catherine's apartment was set up like that. To leave the front room, which was the living room, we had to go through a bedroom that had no doors, into a kitchen and through the kitchen to another bedroom.

We were on the first floor. The kitchen stove had a kerosene burner attached. In the cellar was a 55 gallon drum and we took turns going to the cellar with a gallon jug for kerosene every day. There was a hot water tank standing in the kitchen that was gas-heated. Saturday night was bath night and when the tub was full we took turns. Some hot water was added when the water in the tub got cold. It was very important to remember to shut off the hot water heater when we were finished as it had no controls.

My cousin Young Lester was younger than me and we slept in the bedroom that was between the kitchen and the living room. We had one big double bed, but the room was so small that we could not walk around the bed. We had to climb over it.

West Side Avenue was a main street that crossed Duncan Avenue near their apartment. There were constant buses and trolleys going up and down West Side Avenue which could take us just about anywhere we wanted to go that we didn't walk to. Aunt Catherine and Uncle Lester did not have a car so that was handy. We walked to the local A & P grocery store on West Side Avenue. My first visit to the A&P store was with Aunt Catherine. I could not get over its size. I thought John Rynn's place in Ballinaglera was big until I saw this store, and it was one of the smaller A&P stores.

I was there only a few days when we had the worst snowstorm that I had ever seen. Nothing was moving for days, no buses or trolleys. There had not been a snowstorm that bad in 50 years.

It was my first Christmas in this country. I did not do any shopping. We had a small Christmas tree and they gave me a cigarette lighter with the brand name "Dunhill" on it. I thought it was great. I smoked Pall Mall cigarettes. They did not have a television or a telephone, but not many homes did at that time. They did have a record player that had a small door in the front that dropped down so you could put in one record at a time. That was off limits to young Lester and myself.

After Christmas I got a job at the Western Electric in South Kearney. It paid 75 cents an hour. Western Electric had leased a building in Jersey City so I could walk to work.

John Kellegher used to come see me from time to time. He and Bessie lived in New York City where John also worked. Old Lester, though, did not like John and John didn't get along with Old Lester, either, and after a while he stopped coming.

As I look back now, I should have kept in touch with John. He was the one who helped me the most to get to the States. I was young and out having fun; he was much older and as time went by we drifted apart. I don't remember when Bessie died.

Young Lester had a lot of friends and we used to play stickball on Duncan Avenue by the school. It was nice to be with the crowd. Young Lester was having dental work done and had appointments every week. He never went to any of them because we were busy with the ball games instead. Eventually he got caught.

I was paying Aunt Catherine $15 a week for room and board, and then I started paying her back for the money she put out for my passage. At the same time I used to send $10 home to my father in every letter that I wrote, about once a month. The 75 cents an hour was well spread out.

After six months at Western Electric, in June, 1948, I got laid off. There was a bar on West Side Avenue near Duncan Avenue. Morris Sullivan was the owner. I would stop in on my way from Western Electric for a few beers. It cost ten cents a glass and the third one was a "blow back" (on the house). Old Morris was a nice guy. Saturday afternoons he had hot dogs or a meat loaf all on the house. We would get together and play a card game called Euchre for a round of beer.

When I got laid off, Morris told me to go to the Safeway stores warehouse on Mercer Street in Jersey City for a job. When I told the shop steward, Charlie Halpin, that Morris sent me down, he sent me helping on the trucks—no physical, no papers to fill out, just tell him your name for the pay check. So in midsummer, 1948, I went from 75 cents an hour at Western Electric to $1.75 per hour at Safeway. I was a rich man.

After some time as a helper on trucks, I was told to go to work in the produce warehouse. I would stay in that job for more than 29 years, and thanks to Morris.

The next year, 1949, was not a good year. I was working steady and making good money but it was the year my father died. I had left my Aunt Catherine's because I wasn't getting along with her husband, Uncle Lester. He was a heavy weekend drinker and was usually drunk from Friday after work until Monday morning. When I left their house, I rented a room in a big house on Mercer Street in another part of Jersey City.

I was there only a few weeks when the Rountrees found out, and they came to see me. My Uncle Tom and Aunt Mary Rountree were real nice people. They had two children: Thomas (Buddy) and Mary. Uncle Tom was my mother's brother all the way from Glengevlin, County Cavan. He drove a bus for Public Service all his life. Aunt Mary was from the town of Cong in County Mayo. They asked me to come live with them on Grant Avenue in Jersey City, and it worked out well. Their son Buddy was a few years younger than I was, but we got along. We had our own bedroom, but this time there were two beds.

After Uncle Tom and Aunt Mary had gotten married, they bought a two-family house on Grant Avenue for $4,000. They had a television and a telephone when I went there. Uncle Tom was easy going and always had a smile on his face. Aunt Mary was "the Boss" and a bit cranky. The television had a six-inch picture tube and a large wooden cabinet that was off limits to everyone but Aunt Mary. The telephone was a four-party line and was also off limits.

Buddy and I had some fun times, and we used to go into New York City every once in a while. Buddy liked the girl next door. Her name was Joan Hackert. He spent a lot of time looking through the Venetian blinds with the lights out.

I bought my first car when I lived there. It was a 1935 Ford and I paid a hundred dollars for it. After I got my license, we were always driving around. I soon graduated from the old '35 Ford to a '41 Plymouth. I kept the Plymouth until I went into the Army in 1951 and sold it to my cousin Margaret's husband, Jack Littleton. They lived in Jackson Heights.

When I got out of the Army in 1953, I went back to live with the Rountrees. After three months there, I got married. Not long after that, Buddy went into the service.

I remember my Aunt Catherine and her husband Lester coming over to give me the bad news about my father. He had been at the Fair Day in Dowra and had had a few pints before coming home. After he got home, he could not go to the bathroom and was in a lot of pain. Our neighbor, Patrick Gilrane, got on his bicycle and pedaled the 20 miles to Drumshambo to get my father a doctor. When Patrick got to Drumshambo, however, the doctor was not home. Patrick got an ambulance to come and get my father and they took him to Manorhamilton Hospital. This whole trip had taken hours. Before they got to the hospital, my father's bladder ruptured and poisoned his whole system. He never recovered. I don't know how many days he lived, but it wasn't long.

I did not have enough money to make the trip back home. With the $1.75 an hour I was earning at Safeway and paying back my passage at the same time, I had not been able to save any money. If I made that trip back to Ballinaglera, I might not have come back. It just wasn't to be.

I worked in the produce warehouse until I went into the US Army in February, 1951. The Korean War was not over yet, but I was assigned to an anti aircraft battery, Battery B, AAA Gun Battalion, and was stationed at Fort Totten, Long Island. I liked the service. They were two good years and I had a lot of fun.

I took my basic training at Fort Dix, New Jersey. It was a cold and wet month of February, 1951. The weather was so cold that when we were out on bivouac, the milk on our cereal would freeze before we could finish it. Then the weather changed and it rained for days. Our tents were flooded and all our clothes were wet. But the bad weather did not stop our long 10-mile march or our daily trips to the firing range. KP was a long day of washing pots and pans. Each soldier washed his own gear in a garbage can filled with water. There was a heater in the can and the hot water got the grease off.

After basic I was sent to Fort Totten, Long Island, for advanced training. I enjoyed the time there. It was a nice building we stayed in. It wasn't a long train ride to New York City and I spent many a night in the 8th Avenue bars. After some time, they transferred the anti-aircraft batteries to locations off camp and I was sent to Nutley, New Jersey. Battery B was stationed in a field on Park Avenue in Nutley. It was there that I met Lorraine McCauley.

Tom & Lorraine as Sweethearts

15

Love and Marriage

❧❀❧

A Girl Named Lorraine

The first time that Lorraine and I met was around the Christmas season of 1952.

I had a friend in the service named Silas R. Bailey who was going out with a girl named Dee Smith. She had a friend named Lorraine McCauley, and that is how we got introduced. Lorraine worked down the road from the camp. Every evening when she got out of work she would walk up Park Avenue. Battery B had a piece of equipment called a tracker head that was designed for tracking airplanes. Every afternoon I would sit on the tracker head and adjust it to Park Avenue and would watch for Lorraine to come home from work. She usually wore a black and white checkered jacket with a white blouse which made her an easy target to find.

We were both engaged to other people at the time. I was going out with a girl from Brooklyn and Lorraine had a boyfriend in Nutley. Both of those relationships ended shortly after we met.

Lorraine lived with Bill and Rose Thompson on Race Street in Nutley. They were not related: Rose's mother had been a close friend of Lorraine's mother. Lorraine was in the same situation as myself, without any parents or grandparents. Her mother died right after she was born and her father had died in the Lyons Veterans Hospital in 1939 when she was just five years old. He had been exposed to gas in World War I and had spent the last years of his life in hospitals and nursing homes.

Bill and Rose had five children who were all younger than Lorraine, who became a great help around that house. After she graduated from high school, Lorraine found work in Newark, NJ, with the telephone company. It was a part time job that paid $30 per week. Once Lorraine started working, Rose started charging her $15 a week in rent, so there wasn't much left after bus fare back and forth to Newark.

It was not a long courtship before we got married. We got along very well and had a lot in common. I bought a 1946 Ford. It was a better car than my first one.

One night Lorraine and I were having a few drinks with Silas Bailey and Dee Smith in a bar on River Road in Lyndhurst. It was a snowy night and there were already a couple of inches on the road. We all decided we wanted to leave this place in Lyndhurst and go to another place in Belleville. Since it was my car I was the chauffeur. The road there makes a sharp L turn and when I stepped on the brakes the car went straight into a brick wall. The only injury was that Lorraine hurt her knee. It was a couple of weeks before I got that old car back from the repair shop. It wasn't too expensive since they weren't charging as high a rate per hour back then.

I missed the old car. To get to Jersey City I had to take three buses—one to Newark and then two more to get to Jersey City. Uncle Tom was always asking me where my car was so I had to make up stories. When I finally got the car back, Lorraine and I were back making the rounds. We used to go to Newark to see my aunt, Sister Teresa Agnes. We also used to go to the Latin Quarter in New York City. I remember since I was in uniform at the time they used to sit us by the kitchen. I was not a good tipper then, either. Another good night out was going to the Route 3 drive-in and a stop at Bud's Hut for something to eat.

There were nights when Rose and Bill Thompson were going out and I would spend time at the house with Lorraine watching television. Of course, old Nanny was sitting right across from us with both eyes open.

One night when I took Lorraine home, she got out of the car by the house and her half slip dropped right down to her shoes. She just stepped out of it and picked it up. It was not my fault. I was not a half slip man. I had other plans.

I do not remember asking Lorraine to marry me, or her asking me for that matter, but the subject must have come up since I bought her an engagement ring. It had to be on sale, if you know what I mean. I had had a great time in the Army and I had spent more than I made. I was separated from active duty on February 8, 1953, and was in Ready Reserve for five years. I went back to live with the Rountrees on Grant Avenue in Jersey City. I now had a longer ride to Nutley on the weekends. I also went back to my old job at Safeway stores in the warehouse in South Kearny.

Lorraine's brother Bob and their Aunt Gertrude lived in Newark and we often went there for dinner from time to time. Lorraine was working at Allstate Insurance then and between the two of us we starting saving some money. We starting talking about getting married and Lorraine picked a date in May as the day. The wedding plans quickly fell into place. We would get married in St. Mary's Church in Nutley and hold the reception at Bill and Rose's house.

On May 9, 1953, Lorraine and myself were married. Buddy Rountree was my Best Man and Rose was Lorraine's Matron of Honor. It was a nice wedding and reception. Money was still tight and we could not afford a honeymoon but we did make a trip to Newark to see my aunt Sister Teresa Agnes. Then it was back to work Monday morning. We went to live in a furnished apartment on the Boulevard in Jersey City and borrowed $60.00 from Household Finance for pots and pans. We did make a trip to the Catskills later that summer and we called this trip our honeymoon.

One night early in our marriage we had Lorraine's brother Bob and Aunt Gert over for dinner. Lorraine cooked chicken and everyone said they loved it, but later on she found out that Bob hated chicken. Our first corned beef dinner was roasted in the oven.... Who knew that it was supposed to be boiled?

Wedding Guests

Uncles, Patrick Gilrane, Tom Rountree, Tom Dolan & Cousin Dan Cruise

Aunts,
Wife of Uncle Patrick,
name unknown,
Mary Rountree
& Mary Dolan

I was still smoking at the time and was having stomach trouble. One day at work I got terrible stomach pains. I finished my shift and when I went home, Lorraine took me to the doctor. He sent me right to the hospital that same day and I had emergency surgery for a ruptured ulcer. I don't remember how long I was off work, but this, too, passed, just another part of that chapter of our lives.

January 21, 1954, was another day I remember. It was the day I became an American citizen. I had my five years residence in the country, which was a requirement, and I had passed a test I don't remember much about. I think my few years in the service helped. My Aunt Mary Rountree and her friend went with me since two witnesses were required. Today when we talk about the day I got my citizenship, Lorraine still gets upset, She said that I told her not to come. I think she was working and I don't remember telling her not to come. At the time I didn't think it such a big deal, but looking back now it was an important day in my life. I can understand why Lorraine gets so upset.

We spent about a year in that furnished apartment before we moved to a two-bedroom apartment on West Side Avenue in Jersey City where the rent was $35 a month. It was a cold water flat which meant we had no heat provided and we had to buy our own furniture. We used space heaters during the winter, but it was a cold place, hard to heat. We spent about a year there before Lorraine got pregnant, so now we had to find a place with heat and hot water.

We found a two-bedroom apartment at 50 Lafayette Street in Jersey City for $65 a month. We had a nice couple for landlords, Jim and Ada Gaskin. Our first son, named Tommy, was born on October 30, 1955. While Lorraine was in the hospital with Tommy, I rented a truck and with the help of Uncle Tom Rountree, moved our furniture into our new apartment so that everything was in place when Lorraine and Tommy were ready to come home.

Our little apartment was small. We were on the second floor of a two-family house but there was only one bathroom and it was on the first floor. Our bedroom was between the living room and the kitchen and you had to walk through it to get to either of the other rooms. There was another small bedroom off the kitchen and this was Tommy's room.

Just a year and a half later Lorraine was pregnant again. The apartment was already getting to be too small. Our first daughter, Maryellen, was born on June 29, 1957, and we began to look for some place bigger to live. Now after only five years of marriage we would have moved three times. Ada liked to push the baby carriage with Tommy in it around the block. She hated to see us move and the day we moved out she went fishing off the pier in Long Branch rather than be there when we left.

In 1958, we bought our first house in Carteret, New Jersey. We had the $500 that Aunt Annie had left to us and that was about it. In May we closed on our house at 656 Roosevelt Avenue. I got a GI mortgage, there was no lawyer at the closing, and the total price of the house was $10,500. Our monthly payment including taxes, principal and interest was $80.00 a month. This was a big increase for us over the $65.00 a month we had been paying Ada and Jim. We ended up living in the Roosevelt Avenue house for the next 25 years.

There were only two rooms on the first floor of our new house: a big kitchen and living room. Upstairs there were two bedrooms and bath on the second floor. Within the year, Lorraine was pregnant again. We had a nice family doctor named Fenick. As we got closer to Lorraine's due date in December (1959), if Doc Fenick was going out shopping he would call our house to let us know.

On December 21, 1959, we had another baby girl that we named Lorraine after "the Boss." Now this house was getting small and we hired a contractor finish the attic and create two more bedrooms.

We had nice neighbors that we became very friendly with, Bill and Pat Aymar. We used to have weekly card games and, like myself, Bill liked his beer. They had kids about the same age as ours and the kids played well together. We got into the practice of playing cards almost every weekend with Pat and Bill, and we took turns buying the beer and hosting the card games.

Just about a year later, Lorraine was pregnant again. On May 28, 1961, the four of us were playing our usual card game when Lorraine went into labor. Pat and Bill stayed with the kids while I took Lorraine to Rahway Hospital. I did not have to stay at the hospital, however, because the doctor told me to go home and come back in the morning. When I got back home, Pat and Bill and I continued our card game. Before long, though, the hospital called. Our second son, Patrick, had just been born.

Around this time I stopped smoking and I had no more stomach problems. Some time later I had an accident at work. I was riding on an electric hand truck when a man in front of me pulling a bread rack stopped suddenly. I could not stop in time and my foot got caught between them. I went for x-rays the next day and I had broken some small bones in my foot. My foot was in a cast for a few weeks and I could not work, so Lorraine went out and got a job, and she never stopped working until she retired.

When I went back to work, I went on the second shift so one of us could be home most of the time with the kids. We got a babysitter to watch the children until Lorraine got home from work. Her name was Mrs. Fisher. I would pick her up before I went to work and Lorraine would take her home. Mrs. Fisher would make me a lot of soup, big pots of soup. Then one day Patrick told her that I threw it down the toilet and that was the end of the soup.

I did a lot of cooking when the kids were in elementary school and they came home for lunch every day. I was off on Fridays so that was my day to get dinner.

We were busy all the time and the years went by fast. We had some good times in the old house. We had a small above-ground pool in the back yard during the summer and had picnics all the time. We did survive the school years, although I must say that they were not always fun.

A bad year for me was 1967. That was the year my brother Bernard died. He was in the hospital for some "routine" back surgery. I don't know what the matter was with his back. He had the operation and hoped to be coming home shortly thereafter. He had a major stroke in the hospital and that was the cause of death. The doctors called it an inter cranial hemorrhage.

Unit 4
Merlin park hospital
Galway

Dear Jomie   5.5.67

I got your letter and I was glad to hear from you. Thanks for the dollars I am feeling alright, I have no pain I improved well since I came into the Hospital. It could be some day next week I will have the operation I dont know which day. With Gods help I will get on good. I heard from Teresa she is keeping alright. She got the oats sowed and I think some of them were to give a day at the potatoes. She is getting 30 schillings a week. She has money enough to keep going. Three cows + three caves they are easey managed in this time of year. I am looking for Insurance, I dont know if I will get any as I had not many stamps, Its a big loss not to have them. After the operation I will not be able to write, as I think my hand will be in plaster for some time. It must be nice to see Lorraine going for her first communion The weather is cold and wintery I have not any more news this time I hope all of you well, love from Bernie

Letters from home

12·6·67.   Unit 4
                           merlin Park Hospital
Dear Tomie.   Galway.
          I got your letter at the week
end and I was glad to hear from you.
I am over tree weeks after the operation
And thank God I am feeling good and
I have no pain. I suffered a good bit
for the most of a week. There was a big
wound in my shoulder. I got the stitishes out
in 10 days and the wound was healed,
in too weeks. I am in plaster, a support
for my arm so that there is no weight
on my shoulder. I dont know how long it
will be left on. I did not like it the
first week. I'm getting one injection every
day. I heard from Teresa last week she is
abright. Those days are very warm, thank
God I am able to sit out in the sun, and
walk around, I had the operaion on

thursday and Saturday I was able
to get out to the toilet. On Monday
I had a expray & I was up for a
coupla hours.
I am not able to tell you how
long I will be in the hospital
I was sorry to hear that Tom Rountree
daughter is not well. I hope in God she
gets well again, Sister Teresa Agnes will
be watching for a letter, so if you get
speaking to her, you will let her know
that I am getting on swell.
Thanks for the dollar you sent me
I hope you and all the familey
are well.
                    Love from Bernie

The last letter
from Bernie

You would think we should be rich by now but we were not. With a mortgage and four small children it was hard to save even then. Again I decided not to go back for the funeral. Looking back now I think it was the wrong decision. This was a real bad time for my sister Teresa and might have been the start of her problem. Some time after this she went to England to meet up with the Rountree girls (cousins). Her condition got worse in England and she had to return to Ireland.

After 29 years, the job that old Morris Sullivan had sent me to was closing up. I went to vocational school in Woodbridge, NJ, to learn how to be a Boiler Fireman. After I completed the course, I got my state license. I started studying refrigeration, and with the help of the Watch Engineers at Finast Warehouse, I was able to get my refrigeration license. I went to work for the operating engineers in 1976 and worked in an AT&T complex until I retired in 1991.

Also in 1976, we had saved some money and bought a four-acre wooded lot with a fresh water stream running through it in Acra, New York, in the Catskills. We had a nice three-bedroom ranch house built and we spent many weekends there. Bill and Rose Thompson and Bill and Pat Aymar would spend a lot of time with us "in the mountains." A few years after it was built, we would open it up in the winter for ski weekends for the kids at nearby Hunter Mountain.

During the 1970s, I was a member of the Carteret First Aid Squad and that took up all of my spare time.

Tommy was the first of our children to get married and leave "the nest" in 1978.

In 1980, we got an offer on our Roosevelt Avenue house that was almost four times what we had paid for it, so we sold it. We bought a nice fixer-upper on Hermann Street in West Carteret, and that house kept me busy for quite a few years.

Patrick was the next of the kids to get married in 1981, and he was followed out the door by Lorrie, who got married in September, 1983. Maryellen would get married in 1989, and then Lorraine and I were right back where we started, just the two of us.

In 1991, we sold the Hermann Street and moved into our place in Acra, NY. We spent the next 10 years there. The Catskill Mountains gets very cold in the winter, so we spent a few winters in Florida. In 2002, we sold the Catskills house, and bought a ranch house back in Carteret. You might say we came full circle.

And that's the way it was.

Tom & Lorraine with their Children & Grandchildren.
The first generations of the "Tommy Dan Tims" in America
(Tommy, Erin, Nikki, Lorrie, Katie, Maryellen, Tommy,
Patrick, Lorraine, Tom, Kelsey, Patrick)

Tom with his sons and grandsons
(Tommy, Tommy, Tom, Patrick, Patrick)

Visits back home

Tom & Theresa
circa 1970

Stuck in the shough,
Wayne & Theresa
waiting for help

Himself & The Boss

Visits back home

Tom Senior
with Tommy
at the gate

Hot Wiskeys
at Rvnns

Sightseeing

Visits back home

Tom, Patrick & Tommy
At the old house

Rynns Grocery Store

Patrick Tom & Theresa

Dinner in Dowra

Visits back home

Maryellen at Aillwee Cave

Schoolmates
Francie & Owen Rynn with Tom

The McPaddens with
Lorraine, "the Yankee"

Theresa with, Maryann,
Frankie and Jim McPadden Sr.

Tom & his old friend
John Palmer

Visits back home

Tom with neighbor
Terri Gilrane

Alice Laughlin, childhood friend
with her son JJ

Gail, Theresa & Tommy Gilrane

Tom with neighbor, Sweedin McPartlin

Frankie McPadden,
Second Cousin

Postscript

In 1983, I married Tom & Lorraine's second daughter, Lorraine (Lorrie) Theresa Gilrane, named after her mother and her aunt who still lived in Ireland and who Lorrie had never met. Four years later, Lorrie and I went to Ireland with Tom as our personal guide. All during the 11-day trip, Tom had me do the driving (on the "wrong" side of the road) while he sat in the back and served as navigator, making sure we experienced Bunratty Village and Castle, the Cliffs of Moher, Blarney Castle, and so many other "tourist" sites that he had seen countless times before.

He also took us to his hometown, Dowra, and spoke in a running commentary on what we were seeing, who we were visiting, telling us the about the family that was living in this house, or the names of those who had lived in the one that was now abandoned. There were too many of the latter. At those where someone still lived, we would get out of the car and walk into the house unannounced and without knocking. Although Lorrie and I were strangers to these people, we were made welcome because we were part of Tom's family. The homeowners there were excited to see Tom again, many of them he had known for their entire lives.

We picked up his sister, Teresa, in Sligo and brought her with us while we stayed in Dowra. She seemed to enjoy Lorrie in particular, having never before met her niece. Teresa didn't like to ride in the car, but she resolutely joined us for the short trips we took through the mountains and to nearby Drumshambo for lunch or the evening hot toddy.

Tom took us all to the family plot in the Fahy Cemetery. On the way down a very tight little road, I drove the car off the side and into the "shough." The bottom of the car got hung up on the stones that lined the ditch and we would have to get towed out. That experience didn't help Teresa's distrust of cars, but she was a trooper during the ordeal, and one of my favorite photos of the trip is standing with her in front of the blue car that sits at an odd angle to the ground, my arm around her shoulder.

Tom went to a local farmhouse where the farmer came and pulled us out with his tractor. He wouldn't take any money for his effort or kindness.

At the cemetery, we cleared weeds growing up around the granite stone that Tom had paid for that bore the family name and the first name of those ancestors he has written about here. It is indeed a small plot, what we would call a "single-wide" grave holding the remains of all his ancestors.

We also visited some of the homes Tom had worked at while a boy, and we drove up the mountain road as far as we could to get an idea of how far he'd had to walk to work the turf bog.

But the most poignant time of the entire trip was when we visited the old homestead. The view from the top of the "driveway" (which was actually only a path) overlooking the Lough Allen valley and the mountain range beyond is truly breathtaking. There are several fields between the Loughy Road and the house site. You can't see the remains of the house or byre from the road since they are now surrounded by trees.

While Lorrie and I explored excitedly, Tom and Teresa were somewhat subdued. It had to be difficult for them to be there again, even though it was not their first visit back since Teresa had left. The thick stone walls of the house were still standing as they had been for probably a couple of hundred years. But the thatch roof was long gone, and there were no windows left. We crawled through an open window to get inside. It was hard to imagine a large family living in these three small rooms, but they had. There was no furniture or anything else left. It had been cleaned out many years earlier.

We gathered some soil from the homestead in a jar and brought it home with us, where we had it encased along with pictures of Tom on his property and gave it to him. A man should never be too far from his native soil.

Lorrie and I have often wished since then that we had taken a tape recorder with us to be able to document everything he told us while on that journey. Lacking that, Lorrie and her two brothers and sister kept encouraging their father to write down his thoughts, to make a journal of what he remembered lest we lose all of that information, family history, and Irish lore.

This has been the result.

Tom is a private man, and doesn't like to talk about things too "personal." He had reservations about mentioning anything that might reflect poorly on anyone else, and wanted to keep the focus of this journal on his youth and life in Ireland.

But the reader should know a few more things.

One of the reasons several of Tom's family members encouraged him to write this story was because he has such a wealth of information about Ireland and Irish life that none of the rest of the family could possibly have, and he lived a part of Irish history that is all but forgotten today. The Gilrane family in Derrinageer didn't have much, and the work they did was for their very survival, using tools and implements that very often they had made themselves. It was a difficult life, but one all too familiar for farming families through the 1940s. Tom tells us today that when he left Ireland as a teenager, one sign of the modernization of Ballinaglera was a threshing machine that was going from farm to farm that automatically separated the grain from the straw, a procedure that he and his father and brother had had to do by hand over a barrel in the byre. Modern mechanical farming was making it's way into Ballinaglera in the late 1940s, and it has never been the same since.

When his brother, Bernard, died in 1967, Tom struggled with the decision of whether to go back to Ireland at that time. His sister, Teresa, was left all alone in the old homestead and had had to deal with all of the details of Bernard's funeral by herself. Teresa had expected her 40-year-old twin to return home from the hospital within a week. His sudden death was a shock to everyone, especially Teresa, and she had only the comfort of her neighbors to help her through.

Tom had a very difficult decision to make: he knew his sister needed him, yet he had a wife and four small children here in the States. They didn't have very much money to spare for a round trip. But how would Teresa manage on her own, and what would happen to the farm if he didn't go back to stay? Should he relocate his young American family to Ballinaglera? All of these questions plagued him when he made the very painful choice to not go back. It is a decision that he has regretted. Teresa managed to live alone in the homestead for five more years, and the farm pastures were rented out to other farmers to graze their cattle on.

In 1972, Teresa ended up in the hospital, She vowed not to return to the homestead alone. It was then that Tom was able to finally return to Dowra, and by the time he reached there, the homestead had been ransacked, stripped of all remaining furniture and valuables. Tom helped Teresa get settled in Sligo, and she has lived there with friends ever since.

Back at the farm, he arranged with the local attorney to have the property put legally in his and Teresa's names, and each year the grazing rights were to be publicly auctioned. Since then, Tom has made the trip back home on a biannual basis to see his sister, settle financial accounts with the overseer of the property, and to visit with his remaining family and friends. Almost every trip back found fewer and fewer of those he knew still alive and living in Ballinaglera.

As a family, we have been instilled with Irish history and lore, all of it coming from Tom. Now 77 years old, he can no longer rent a car when he visits Ireland (the cut-off is 75 years of age) so he'll only go when he can get a driver to go with him. His children all have families of their own, and it isn't easy for us to find the time or the money to go when he wants to. But he is very patient about it.

Tom's roots are still deeply embedded in Ireland. He carries a pencil that has usually been sharpened by a penknife. He cringes when he hears the oil burner come on to bring heat into his house since the oil is something that has to be paid for. He even uses Dowra as part of his email address. And God forbid that you waste hot water in his presence. "You know, in my day, we had to carry water up to the house, and then heat *it on the turf fire. We never wasted hot water." It wasn't a rebuke as much as it was a reminder.*

Some habits are just too ingrained to ever change.

In recent months, we have been exploring the possibility of restoring the old homestead, but the distance and money involved have kept that dream at bay. Some day, some day …

Now retired, Tom and Lorraine usually summer in the Irish region of the Catskills in East Durham, New York. There they spend their days and evenings with other Irish men and women swapping stories, sharing pictures of the grandchildren, playing cards, and just plain enjoying the company of like-minded folks. You know, their own form of rambling. Their love of Ireland is never far from the surface. You can hear it through their brogue as they speak. It's a love affair with a distant land that not enough of us can appreciate.

It is just the way it is.

Wayne T. Dilts

978-0-595-44711-4
0-595-44711-2

Printed in the United States
90500LV00009B/184-189/A